Praise for THE CANADIAN GARDENER by Marjorie Harris with photographs by Tim Saunders:

"[THE CANADIAN GARDENER] is perhaps the best gardening book of its kind ever published in Canada."

Edmonton Journal

"Hands-on gardeners should raise hymns of gratitude. I could not find a single practical point which [Harris] did not treat."

Toronto Life

"In THE CANADIAN GARDENER, Harris successfully brings both her artistic vision and practical knowledge to enrich the understanding of both the beginner and expert gardener."

Vancouver Sun

"The prose is written in a manner that is exactly like [Marjorie] Harris: a barrel of fun, but up and working at the crack of dawn."

Toronto Star

"An eminently readable, helpful and beautifully photographed book on Canadian gardening."

Canadian Gardening

"The book's greatest strength is the emphasis that it gives to the wide diversity of designs available for Canadian gardens."

Maclean's

ECOLOGICAL GARDENING

The
CANADIAN GARDENER
ECOLOGICAL
GARDENING
YOUR PATH TO A HEALTHY GARDEN

by Marjorie Harris

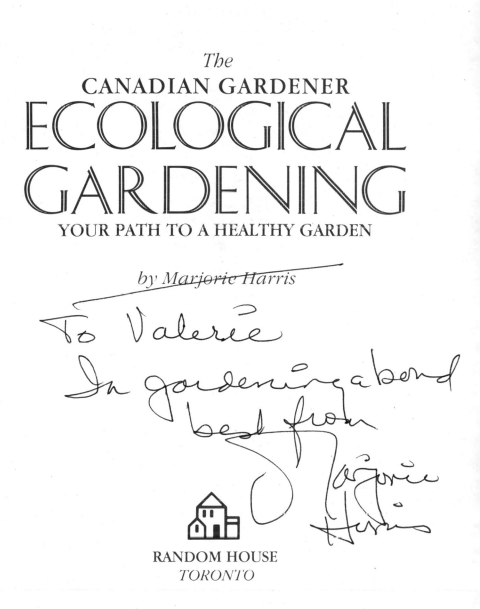

To Valerie

In gardening a bond best from

Marjorie Harris

RANDOM HOUSE
TORONTO

For Amanda and Laurie
and the members of Grassroots Albany
who are serious about the survival of this
beautiful planet

Published in Canada in 1991 by
Random House of Canada Limited, Toronto.

Printed on paper
containing over 50%
recycled paper including
5% post-consumer fibre.

Canadian Cataloguing in Publication Data

Harris, Marjorie
Ecological gardening

(The Canadian gardener)
ISBN 0-394-22199-0

1. Organic gardening – Canada.   2. Garden ecology –
Canada.   I. Title.   II. Series: Harris, Marjorie.
The Canadian gardener.

SB453.5.H37 1991   635'.0484'0971   C90-095428-0

Design and art direction: Andrew Smith
Editorial: Barbara Schon
Cover illustration: Audra Geras
Line illustrations: David Chapman

Printed and bound in Canada

10 9 8 7 6 5 4 3 2 1

CONTENTS

ACKNOWLEDGEMENTS

Thanks to Diane Martin of the Ecological Agriculture Projects of Macdonald College and to all the wonderful articles written by Dr. Stuart B. Hill, the guru of soil; Murray Haigh, Mary Perlmutter, Canadian Organic Growers, Juliet Mannock, Amanda McConnell, Marge Stibbards, Anna Leggatt and Judith Adam. And Barbara Schon who does such a fantastic job of editing these books.

INTRODUCTION

W E NOW KNOW THAT THE EARTH IS ONE VAST LIV-
ing, breathing system where everything relates to
everything else. It fits together in the most delicate and
beautiful way. The ecological garden is a metaphor for
planet earth—reflecting this finely tuned, integrated
whole.

To become an ecological gardener, you will have to
understand how your garden functions at the most basic
level, that is, the relationship between the soil, light, air and
the plants you use in your garden. You'll become extremely
sensitive to the environment, and less haphazard in your
approach to the earth. The more exhausted the planet
becomes, the more important it is to put back almost
everything we take from it.

And it's exciting to figure out the composition of soil,
what plants need, and how to put them together for a
healthy, pest-resistant garden. On top of these benefits is
the delight in watching how your own caretaking abilities
expand. Even the slightest understanding of how all elements in nature mesh together adds to the pleasure of
gardening.

In this book I've looked at the fundamentals of organic
gardening: the soil and how it functions; insects—good and
bad; pests; weather; diseases; weeds; mulching. We need to
use alternatives to the chemicals we've been putting into
the biosphere for too many years now. Ecological gardening is, in many ways, a return to a simpler form of gardening—a retrieving of wisdom. Many of the ancient ways are

far more effective than the currently popular high-tech solutions.

We must take the greenhouse effect very seriously. There is more and more evidence that the burning of fossil fuel increases atmospheric gas that leads, in turn, to increased temperatures. A surplus of carbon dioxide might alter the architecture of some plants; cell chemistry might evolve to a less efficient use of water in plants. We just don't know. And we don't know the long-term consequences. We do know that cycles of drought may increase in some areas, and torrents of rain increase in others where it's not expected. We're going to have to think about these things when we approach gardening.

Here are some of the basics to get you started on ecological gardening:

1. Treat the soil, not the plant is the litany of all organic gardeners. Improve your soil organically with compost and humus of your own making. It's the cheapest and best form of nutrition.
2. Get the hardiest plants, ones most resistant to disease. Or, instead of buying expensive hybrids, use species plants. These are the closest ones to those found in the wild and most likely to survive the assault of our weather extremes.
3. Choose native plants. They have a genetic factor that has allowed them to survive drought, fierce winters, wind or excessive rain over hundreds of thousands of years.

Start here and then move on to the other suggestions contained in this book. It won't take long. Within two years you'll find that gardening is a lot more fun. By not buying a lot of chemicals, you'll actually be saving yourself a fair whack of money. And you'll be doing the planet a giant favor.

CHAPTER ONE

SOIL: THE REAL DIRT

❧

I BECAME AN ORGANIC GARDENER LONG BEFORE I knew what the term meant. When I started gardening twenty-odd years ago, labels on fertilizer packages with 10-10-10 or 2-10-whatever baffled me. These products all seemed to be manufactured by the big chemical companies I was, no doubt, boycotting because of their involvement in the Vietnam war. Since I was composting out of habit and the garden seemed healthy enough, I didn't bother with synthetic fertilizers. Through laziness I was doing exactly what I should have been. Ecological gardening by default.

The most important philosophical gardening question to ask yourself is this: What is the nature of soil? Think for a moment how we even acquired this miraculous substance. Over millions of years, great upheavals around the world exposed huge rocks, then glacial movement scoured them clean. In the retreat of the great ice ages, moraines, boulders and clay were left behind. They became deposits of gravel and sand as they were pounded away by the action of wind and rain. Over the eons, through the action of bacteria, fungi, lichens, arthropods and eventually earthworms, a thin layer of soil emerged.

In fact the earth you stand on in your garden seethes with life. Imagine big animals devouring little animals, great migrations, the drama of birth and death all going on in a dark world that requires oxygen and water to survive. Sounds very much like what happens on top of the soil, doesn't it? Though we are very concerned about the quality

1

of our air, we seldom think about this other part of the biosphere.

Half the soil consists of solid material, mostly mineral particles, and half consists of spaces between; and half of these, in turn, are filled with water that occurs as a film around the particles. All these microscopic bits and pieces are so vital that without them the soil would be sterile. And we would be doomed.

What's taking place in this subterranean world is a cycle of death and decomposition of one organism for the feeding of others. Eventually these death throes supply all the nutrients needed by plants. The ultimate in recycling.

The most devastating part of all of this is that we are ill-informed about these relationships and even the cleverest of scientists doesn't know the whole story. And most of us seldom think about soil at all. This life is churning away beneath our feet and yet every move we make serves to kill it off. Our prairies once had the most fertile soil in the world, an extraordinary humus created over thousands of years. We've managed to deplete it in a century with one-crop farming, ripping out the native grasses that held it in place, leaving it exposed to the elements, and allowing humongous compacting machinery to roll over it. All this conspires to kill the life below the surface. Add the assault of chemical fertilizers almost non-stop for 40 years plus pollution, fires, floods and you'll begin to understand what's happening to this fragile world.

The microscopic animals of the soil live a full life if they are allowed to. They browse, swim, travel, have profligate sex lives, procreate and die providing food for the big guys—arthropods and earthworms. The symbiosis between these animals is highly structured. What happens when we interfere chemically with all this activity is that we slowly poison the soil by killing off mites, bacteria, fungi and, even worse, earthworms. The remaining species multiply. This throws off the balance entirely. The level of chemicals will steadily increase until the soil becomes toxic to plants, animals and people.

What keeps the soil healthy are all these organisms in the perpetual process of decomposition: dying matter breaks down into humus and through this, releases nutrients for plants. When we put the soil in jeopardy, our very survival is in question.

Dr. Stuart B. Hill, the Soil Guru of Canada, says that rather than killing off bacteria and fungi, we should be investigating and developing management strategies for their productive potential.

"Such strategies," he maintains, "are likely to save money, energy, and avoid damage to the support environment and to human and livestock health. This contrasts with our current approach, which involves the removal of several dozen minerals at harvest time followed by the replacement of only a few of them as chemical fertilizers." (*Agricultural Chemicals and the Soil* [1977]).

Pests and diseases are generally considered symptoms of poor management by bioagriculturists. Pesticides, antibiotics and drugs have generally been regarded as "magical bullets" that can eliminate problems. "The real situation," Dr. Hill says, "is that we do not suffer from pests because of a deficiency of pesticide in the environment just as we do not get a headache because of a deficiency of aspirin in the blood." Keep that line in mind when you get into an argument with a chemical pusher.

This dependency on chemicals *is* much like an addiction. The more you use, the more you need to merely survive. But the depletion of soil expands exponentially. And what little short-term gain there is for the private person will eventually become a huge public burden to try and recover the health of our soil.

3

The soil has amazing strategies of its own for dealing with the things that are harmful. For instance, there are nematodes that are dreadful killers. They get into the roots of plants and suck them dry. But to counter this, there are fungi that strangle the bad nematodes. And most other nematodes are helpful to the soil.

To give you an idea of just how complex all of this is, there may be a hundred thousand protozoa in the water that surrounds a few particles of soil. The millions of bacteria in each gram of soil are crucial to decomposition. And to aid the process, there's the activity of earthworms.

EARTHWORMS

Aristotle referred to earthworms as the intestines of the earth and Darwin to them as nature's ploughmen. Earthworms, Darwin calculated, could move 7.5 to 18 tons of soil per acre (0.4 ha) annually.

Our earthworms are thought to have been pretty much done in by the last ice age. One of the few favors Europeans did when they came to this continent was bring earthworms with them. There are now 19 recorded species in Canada of which 18 are primarily European. Earthworms eat up the fallen leaves and start the whole decomposition process, though they won't work on fresh beech or oak with the same efficiency as on other leaves. They gobble up organic matter and leave behind castings filled with calcium, potassium and phosphorus; stir up the soil and bring nutritional material closer to the surface and accessible to plants; aerate the soil through burrows that bring oxygen to the bacteria that need it to survive. These burrows are also channels for roots and increase the ability of water to move through the soil.

Worms aid in creating the all-important humus. They hate anything that messes with soil life—especially synthetic fertilizers. So we should be aware of their value. In healthy soil there will be about 300 earthworms in each square yard (metre). I'm not suggesting that you count them, but in anything but acid soil, however, if you haven't got a lot of wormy activity, you've got a problem.

KNOW YOUR SOIL

No doubt there is a Platonic form that contains the perfect soil: dark loam containing enough beautifully balanced humus to hold just the right amount of rain but with excellent drainage. It's out there somewhere but what most of us are usually presented with has something wrong with it: too heavy, too sandy, too much clay and always, always the possibility of past over-cultivation. This can happen in a few seasons if nothing organic is put back into the soil. What your soil probably needs is some form of conditioning.

Fertile soil is a cumulative process, one of continuous improvement. Two things are required: humus and finely ground rock particles. The latter make up the mineral portion of the soil. But it is the humus or organic matter which is most important. Dr. Hill refers to the process as a primitive form of farming that's been going on for 400 million years. What keeps the farm thriving is decomposition of organic matter.

Organic matter comprises living matter, such as leaves, in the process of decay. To break down, leaves need many different fungi, each with a special function, to attack them. Then there are mites and other arthropods that come next. If you destroy any of these with pesticides, you can upset the balance needed for proper decomposition. Since most of these creatures are beneficial, it seems unnecessary to go on a rampage of chemical warfare for the few that might not be beneficial. You might also destroy their natural predators which can, in turn, overgraze and reduce any short-term good the chemicals might provide.

There are organisms like the mycorrhizal fungi that perform herculean tasks in the soil. They not only improve plant health, they also help plants absorb phosphorus, which is essential to growth, and assimilate trace elements, which assist plants in withstanding the stress of drought. Experiments are now under way in how to use these fungi as an inoculum. And what do they need to prosper? In its simplest form—aerated soil with lots of organic matter. But they won't co-operate if pesticides and herbicides have been used.

FEED THE SOIL

The more intimate you are with your soil, the better handle you'll have on dealing with any problems that arise. To feed the soil, you need to know what the menu should be.

THE STRUCTURE OF SOIL • Soil comes in layers. Depending on how great your soil is, each layer will be from a few inches (centimetres) to a few feet (metres). It comes from the bedrock of the earth and is like a thin skin on its surface. It takes about 500 years to create one inch (2.5 centimetres) of soil through weathering.

The texture of soil depends on the sand, clay and silt content. Ideal soil is 25 percent water, 25 percent air and the balance organic matter: all the animals and micro-organisms that live there plus minerals. In this same ideal soil micro-organisms release 3 pounds (1.3 kilograms) of nitrogen a year, which is about the equivalent of a 50-pound (23 kilogram) bag of 6-10-4 commercial fertilizer. All of the nitrogen and sulphur, and one-third of the phosphorus and other nutrients are supplied by organic matter.

Humus: The top layer of organic matter in the process of decaying is humus. It helps the soil absorb water, provides air spaces critical to plant development, and is filled with the nutrients plants need for survival.

Topsoil: This is where the life of your soil is found. Earthworms, bacteria and a multitude of other animal organisms live here. It contains minerals and organic matter ranging from 49 percent to 1 percent depending on the location. The depth could be from a fraction of an inch (a few millimetres) to 18 inches (45 centimetres) or more.

Subsoil: There are fewer nutrients at this level. But soil conditioning can help a shallow subsoil. The material here is pulverized and there's no humus.

Hardpan: This is self-descriptive. Clay and silt make it almost impermeable. At this level there is little or no drainage. Minerals are not added from this depth. The closer to the surface you find hardpan, the more shallow-rooted the plants will be.

Bedrock: There is no soil below this level.

TYPES OF SOIL • To evaluate your soil, take a chunk of earth out in a square approximately 12 inches (30 centimetres) deep. Now pull a fistful from the centre of the batch. Moisten it slightly and then rub it over your hand to figure out what type of soil you have.

Heavy: Scrunch up the moistened soil, and it will hold the shape of your hand. Clay contains most of the nutrients but has very few spaces between the tiny particles. That means it has poor drainage and is slow to warm up in the spring. It needs to be lightened up with organic matter, such as humus or compost, plus sand, for improved drainage.

Perfect: Loam comprises 40 percent sand, 40 percent silt, 20 percent clay. It's great stuff. Has the famous balance, and when it's wet you can make a ball that falls apart easily. It drains readily. This is what, ideally, you are aiming for. Once you have loam, keep adding compost or humus to keep it up to scratch.

Light: Mainly sandy. Very gritty stuff with large particles that let water drain away far too quickly. This kind of soil needs an underlying level of humus or organic matter such as well-rotted leaves.

Mixed: Silty loam feels smooth and forms a weak ring. Sandy loam is gritty and forms a ball but not a cylinder. If you have a soggy mess of mucky peat soil that just sort of plops in the hand, it needs serious amending.

SOIL TESTING • If you're unsure whether you have acid or alkaline soil have it tested at a garden centre, agricultural station or soil laboratory. See pages 17-18 for some suggestions. Otherwise try local nurseries, horticultural centres or botanical gardens. There are also kits available that are relatively efficient.

To prepare a soil test: Dig a sample from every 100 square feet (9 square metres) to a depth of 6 to 12 inches (15 to 30 centimetres). Mix the sample in a bucket and send about a pint (1/2 litre) of this mix to be tested. If you describe what you want to plant, the soil can be tested for that purpose. You will be given the nutrient content, pH and a description of texture. On a scale of 0 to 14 here's how your soil will stack up:

Acid soil – below 7 pH — A fast way to figure out if you have acid soil is to take a small amount and add a bit of vinegar. If the vinegar sizzles, you've got alkaline soil. If not, that means there's acid in it and the vinegar (itself an acid) won't react with it. Weeds will let you know if you have acid soil: meadow foxtails; daisies; mouse-ear hawkweed; corn marigold or corn chrysanthemum, *Chrysanthemum segetum*; corn spurry; sheep sorrel, sow-thistle, coltsfoot and nettles. Masses of Johnny-jump-ups may also indicate acidity.

FOR PLANTS NEEDING ACID SOIL • If you don't have acid soil but want to plant acid-loving plants such as rhododendrons, azaleas and heaths, try the following:
- Dig out a bed to 18 inches (45 centimetres) deep and fill with a mixture of: sharp sand and garden loam to 3 parts acid peat; sawdust from pines or oak; add 5 pounds (2 kilograms) sulphur per 100 square feet (3 square metres).
- Once the acid-loving plant is in place, add 2 teaspoons (10 grams) powdered sulphur every square foot.

Maintenance:
- Dig sphagnum peat into the area and allow it to winter over. When you are using peat, you must soak it with hot water and let it sit if it's to add any moisture-retention qualities to the soil.
- Keep out the earthworms since their castings include calcium. Don't use bone meal or wood ashes—both contain lime.
- Check out the rainwater (for instance, around the Toronto region our rain is getting more and more acid—pollution).
- Mulch with leaf mould from oaks and pines. Don't cultivate these plants.
- Limestone helps maintain the pH level in the liveliest range of activity, between 6.2 and 6.8. It also supplies calcium and magnesium.

NEUTRAL SOIL - 6.0 TO 8.0 • Most plants like to grow within this range and you have only to maintain its health with proper mulching and fertilizing (See chapter 3).

ALKALINE SOIL - ABOVE 7.0 • Some soils are too alkaline and most plants like a neutral soil, between 6.0 and 7.0. Weeds indicating alkalinity: white mustard, clustered bellflower, musk thistle, black knapweed, Queen-Anne's lace, salad burnet and henbane.

REMEDIES • If soil is too alkaline, try the following:
• Add sulphur if you're in a rare area that doesn't suffer from acid rain. It will lower the pH if it's too high for what you want to plant.
• Other materials that will lower the pH are calcium sulphate and aluminum sulphate.
• Compost will make a soil more neutral if you add about 2 to 3 inches (5 centimetres to 7.5 centimetres) a year.
• Lime will reduce acidity. Dolomitic limestone contains magnesium and calcium thus fertilizing the soil at the same time, so it is the recommended form. Apply in the fall after the ground is dug or ploughed, to give it a chance to break down—which it does very slowly.
• Wood ashes will act faster to reduce acidity since they are about 20 to 50 percent calcium carbonate. They are high in phosphorus. The best time to apply is late winter or early spring, but never near germinating seeds.

WHAT'S IN A SOIL • The three major components of soil are nitrogen, phosphorus and potassium. These are the NPK on fertilizer bags—some things eventually get through—if it's a 21-7-7 that means it contains 21 percent nitrogen, 7 percent each of phosphorus and potassium.

There are vital interrelations between all the elements in the soil—once again it's your job to maintain the delicate balance.

The other major elements in the soil are: carbon, hydrogen, oxygen, calcium, magnesium and iron. Then there are the trace elements: boron, copper, manganese, zinc, molybdenum, sulphur and zinc. These are the hardest to manipulate so concentrate on the major elements.

Nitrogen is released when soil organisms decompose. When a plant dies, most of the nutrients taken out of the soil are returned to the soil. This in turn is transformed into humus (dark porous substance which contains the acids that make other nutrients available to plants). Nitrogen production increases under warm, moist conditions and slopes off when circumstances begin to cool. Nitrogen is needed for vegetative plant growth.

Organic matter in the soil is crucial for soil microorganisms to release nitrogen. Leaf mould, compost, manure, dead roots and plants, insects and animals, the minutiae of the soil—bacteria and fungi (carried upwards by the ever-vigilant earthworms)—are all organic matter. The ultimate goal of this decaying process is the production of humus—the most superb type of organic matter you can build for your soil. When you walk through the woods some day, lift some moss or rotting leaves. The marvellous sticky black stuff under them is humus. The process of decomposition has been completed and it is feeding the soil. This is the material that will heal your soil if it's sick. Sources of nitrogen:

- Fish emulsion.
- Blood meal—has a nitrogen content of 8 to 13 percent.
- If you use manure to bump up the nitrogen content of your soil, I recommend sheep manure—it has a higher nitrogen content than other types. Use manure that's

11

been composted (so that the heating process will kill off any weed seeds) for at least six months.
- Manure will also improve soil texture.
- Finished compost is an excellent source of nitrogen.

The beauty of these products is that they release nitrogen slowly and naturally—usually as the plants need it. They aren't going to burn the plants or you.

Synthetic forms of nitrogen have a much higher nitrogen content but take a good look at them. Anhydrous ammonia is about 82 percent nitrogen. But if you breathe it, you can die. If it gets too close to the root system of a plant, it causes damage. Urea has 45 percent nitrogen but if it's mishandled, plants will die. Most chemical fertilizers with high nitrogen content are taken up by plants so quickly that they produce initial lush growth which is watery and weak, and the plants are easily broken off by the wind. They are also more susceptible to disease.

Phosphorus is needed for fruit development, root growth, resistance to disease and to help withstand stress. Mix any of the following with manure and dig in in spring. This element doesn't leach out easily and is released into the soil slowly.
Sources of phosphorus include:
- Colloidal phosphate—18 to 25 percent phosphoric acid. Use every four years.
- Rock phosphate and greensand have long been recommended, but if they come from North America they'll contain uranium.
- Bone meal.
- The jury is still out on superphosphate. It's rock phosphate processed with sulphuric acid. I try to keep away from products that require a lot of energy in their production. But when I have used this I've been pleased— but guilty of course.

- Rock and colloidal phosphate will raise the soil pH making it less acid.
- When you are using rock minerals, use them in a natural form. By doing this, you will avoid getting into the problem of excessive mineralization or the leaching out of soluble elements—which could affect ground water. Balance is everything. When the temperature rises and the soil is moist, these nutrients will become available to the plants much more quickly.

Potassium is needed for growth. Helps a plant resist disease, protects from cold and from excessive loss of water.

- Too much magnesium in the soil will lead to a potassium deficiency.
- Wood ashes (from the fireplace not the barbecue). Be careful—they can boost the pH, and if it gets too high you'll succeed in killing off your acid-loving plants.
- Manure, with sheep and goat having the highest content (3 percent).
- Straw.

Micronutrients such as manganese, iodine, zinc, iron, copper, boron and molybdenum are all in the soil and if they aren't, your plants will let you know something is wrong. Lots of organic matter worked into the soil will correct any imbalances. It contains these trace elements and is the simplest, safest way to a healthy soil.

SOIL AMENDING

Make your soil self-sufficient by making it healthy. You don't want to provide merely a temporary solution to your soil problems. Manure and organic matter aren't necessarily interchangeable in organic gardening. Organic matter is the most important: leaves, plant waste, garden detritus, straw, hay.

Another method of enriching the soil: dig down deeper and fill with compost; layer with aged leaves, manure; add earthworms (from your collection in a box filled with peat moss, compost, leaves, coffee grounds). The earthworms do most of the work.

Build up the soil with compost or make your own organic fertilizer as recommended by Eliot Coleman: four parts of blood meal, two parts bone meal, and one part kelp or rock phosphate.

Soil Food from *Organic Gardening for the Pacific Northwest*: 4 parts seed meal (or 2 parts fish meal); 1 part dolomitic limestone; 1 part rock phosphate or ½ part bone meal; 1 part kelp.

- If you add bone and blood meal to peat moss, it will be a fertilizer. Peat on its own is sterile.
- Leaf mould: Bag leaves and leave them in a corner to break down, or dig them into a big hole and let them rot, or shred them and add to the compost. One thing you don't do with leaves is throw them out. Maple leaves as a mulch tend to mat if you put them on without letting them break down first. Norway maples especially should be well composted since the leaves contain alkaloids.
- Oak and beech are acidic and will take longer to break down than other leaves but are great if you are building up acid areas in your garden.
- Black walnut leaves and areas around these trees are poisonous.

Sandy soil: Really sandy soil is too porous and it won't support earthworms. Add clean clay-fired Kitty Litter in each planting hole, then add soil amenders. The Kitty Litter will absorb water, cutting down on the need for excessive watering. Don't use the kind with deodorized crystals.

SOLVING SOIL PROBLEMS

If you have soil with poor texture or density, try the following:

Double dig: Dig a trench as wide as your spade, and as deep. Pile the soil from the first trench on a sheet of plastic. Dig another trench; put this soil in the first trench, and so on until you hit the last trench and then put the soil on the plastic sheet from the first in it.

Raised beds: Double dig an area 5 feet square (150 centimetres). Add enough peat and compost or manure to raise it a few inches. Sphagnum peat is acid; always soak it first for a few days.

BUYING TOPSOIL

If you must buy bagged soil, be careful. Try to find out where it came from. If it's from a field that was planted with corn, it may be filled with toxic chemicals. In that case, don't buy it. Of course it may be from the nearest new housing development. Sometimes the valuable topsoil is removed and sold, leaving new homeowners with nothing but subsoil and clay. If you're in this latter position, bump up the soil first before you go through the heartbreak of putting in a garden and watching it struggle. Usually the sod that's put in will last for a few years but you'll have to use masses of compost and manure on it to keep it viable. Don't be tempted by quick solutions.

Eliot Coleman's organic potting mix:

20 quarts black peat	20 L
1/2 cup dolomitic lime	125 mL
Mix, and add	
20 quarts coarse sand	20 L
20 quarts brown peat	20 L
1 cup colloidal phosphate	250 mL

1 cup greensand	250 mL
1 cup blood meal	250 mL
Mix, and add	
10 quarts soil	10 L
10 quarts compost	10 L

Prepare three months in advance (reduces the possibility of blood meal bringing on a nitrate reaction).

Lead in the soil: Lead in the soil may come from leaded paint or residues of leaded gas from nearby cars. By adding lots of compost and manure, you can decrease lead absorption. By maintaining neutral soil of 6.5, you'll also be able to limit the build-up of lead in the soil.

Rocky soil: If you do have a lot of rocks on your property, they can be recycled into the garden. Back up plants that like hot dry conditions with large rocks. Place smooth flat rocks near plants that like cool moist conditions—I put them over the roots of clematis, for instance.

I don't mess around cultivating the soil once it's been planted. I like to think I'm not disturbing the complex life that exists down there. After all, the most beneficial life is in just slightly over the top inch (3 centimetres).

To create a healthy, balanced soil in your ecological garden, use every alternative to cultivating you can find. Be sure to mulch and otherwise keep the soil covered. If you want to see what will happen when you fail to protect the soil, take a chunk of bare earth and aim your hose at it. It will turn to sand very quickly. Return what you take from the garden to the garden (leaves, dead and dying plants—unless they are diseased). Feed with organic matter. Compost, compost, compost.

- Make sure you know what kind of soil and drainage you have and work with it or amend it to accommodate the plants you want to grow. Find out what was added to

your soil before you took possession. If it's been stripped of topsoil, if chemicals have built up in the soil, you will have to bump up the soil over a period of time.
• Plant when it's good for the plant and bad for pests.
• A handy way to inoculate your soil against diseases is to plant marigolds, and then rotate them from year to year. Another bonus—rodents don't like them either.

Learn to treasure the soil and approach it as a living creature rather than some dead stuff you clunk plants into. The more you are aware of the symbiosis between yourself and the soil, the more careful you will be of this miraculous substance.

Soil Testing Labs: Be sure to request organic results. You won't get them in every case, but it's a good idea to keep up the pressure.

Newfoundland and Labrador:
Soil and Land Management Division
Provincial Agriculture Building
P.O. Box 4750
St. John's, Nfld. A1C 5T7

Prince Edward Island:
P.E.I. Dept. of Agriculture
Soil and Feed Testing Laboratory
P.O. Box 1600, Research Station
Charlottetown, P.E.I. C1A 7N3

Nova Scotia:
Soils and Crops Branch
Nova Scotia Dept. of Agriculture and Marketing
P.O. Box 550
Truro, N.S. B2N 5E3

New Brunswick:
Plant Industry Branch
Dept. of Agriculture
P.O. Box 6000
Fredericton, N.B. E3B 5H1

Quebec:
Nutrite
Box 1000
Brossard, Que. J4Z 3N2

Ontario:
Nutrite
Box 160
Elmira, Ont. N3B 2Z6

Manitoba:
Manitoba Provincial Soil Testing Laboratory
Dept. of Soil Sciences
Room 262, Ellis Building
University of Manitoba
Winnipeg, Man. R3T 2N2

Saskatchewan:
Saskatchewan Soil Testing Laboratory
Dept. of Soil Science
General Purpose Building
University of Saskatchewan
Saskatoon, Sask. S7N 0W0

Alberta:
Alberta Soils and Animal Nutrition Laboratory
905, Longman Building
6909-116, NW. St.
Edmonton, Alta. T6H 4P2

British Columbia:
Griffin Labs Corp.
1875 Spall Road
Kelowna, B.C. V1Y 4R2

CHAPTER TWO

COMPOSTING: GARDEN GOLD

❧

MY FAMILY ALWAYS HAD A COMPOST PILE OF SOME sort, however primitive, and I was appalled to find that this was not a universal practice. I built my first one when we bought this house in the 1960s—just as soon as we'd pulled the 3x19x120 feet (1x6x36 metres) of weeds out of the backyard. My neighbor, objecting to what he termed throwing out garbage and making flies, called city hall. When the health inspector arrived, he hooted with laughter, "About the only thing you're making is a lot of worms." The compost kept Steve and me at odds for years. It was like two politically opposed people—neither could possibly understand the other's point of view.

The value of composting has become increasingly clear. It cuts down on garbage to an enormous degree. It puts back what you take out of the environment. Recycling at its best. And you can start any time of the year. The more I work with and read about compost, the more I realize I have to learn. On our street, we're lucky to have Amanda to keep us informed. She's been dubbed our "Mistress of Composting" and is willing to give annual refresher seminars to those of us who can't seem to remember what we're doing from one minute to the next.

Without going on and on about its virtues, remember this: compost is even better than well-rotted manure. Manure will, of course, amend your soil beautifully. But it isn't a complete fertilizer. Compost is—plus it's the most nutritious hit there is for your soil. The microorganisms that build up in it supply what is comparable in humans to an inoculation against disease or to an antibiotic if you've got a disease. It will improve both the aeration and drainage of your soil as it supplies nutrients. And it's free. Need I go on?

What is compost? It's organic matter broken down by bacteria and other organisms into a dark material called humus. It feels like the most perfectly wonderful soil imaginable.

To give you an idea of how easy it is to compost, when you mow a lawn and leave the clippings in place, you are composting; when you let leaves stay on the ground to rot, you are composting. But to compost on a more sophisticated level, you have to put a bit of effort into it.
• You need some form of container,
• you need to layer what you put into it,
• you need to keep it relatively moist (not wet),
• you need to turn it occasionally.

If you follow those simple rules, you will have good compost and it will not smell. What creates a stink is throwing in all of one thing: nothing but kitchen waste, nothing but leaves, nothing but grass clippings. Gases build up, ergo, nasty smell. By layering, the stack heats up and cooks the smell out. I can get quite intoxicated by compost odor. When it has a slight earthy smell, which I love, that means it's a success. It's a sensual pleasure to plunge an arm into it and let the lovely stuff run through your fingers.

The scientific basis of all composting is that organic matter is valuable only while decaying and even finished compost still has a way to go in that process. It's this process that provides nutrients to the soil. Microscopic bacteria and other minuscule organisms continually assimilate organic material releasing the nutrients plants need.

Bacteria alone are 60 percent protein. These provide food for the munchers you can see: worms, insects such as sow bugs, nematodes, mites and so on. They eat, digest, excrete and die. As this happens, more and more nutrients are released. When you see all that life, the visible and invisible, the creepies and crawlies in your compost—talk about teeming with life—they are all working for you.

The red worms that develop in compost heaps are special worms that don't live in the earth. They are smaller, very red and live only in compost. They create air passages, providing the environment for the oxygen-loving organisms. Carbon dioxide and water are produced, both of which are odorless. When the compost heats up during the decomposition process, these special worms won't die. And they seem to appear like magic once you provide the right kind of environment for them.

There are two types of decaying processes: **aerobic** and **anaerobic**.

- Aerobic composting is with air or oxygen which feed oxygen-loving bacteria and spur them on with the work of decomposition.
- Anaerobic is without air; decay is slower; gases are formed and probably the pile will end up smelling like rotten eggs. Primarily carried on in closed bins or silos.

Aerobic is the best and most efficient, but it means getting oxygen into the heap by turning it. Leave a post in the centre to wiggle or use another ingenious method we'll discuss below.

LOCATION

A compost heap needs good drainage so don't build it on top of concrete or in an area where water won't run off.

Give it a shady spot so it won't dry out, but where the sun might hit it at some time, though this is not terribly important. Use a cover to keep animals out, and keep it as damp as a squeezed-out sponge—neither soggy nor dry.

An excellent place to locate a compost bin or pile is about six feet (2 metres) away from a birch or elder tree. You'll miss the dripline and worms adore both these trees.

HOW TO GET STARTED

Use the container that suits the size of your garden best. I have a relatively small garden, so I like the Soilsaver, a heavy-duty prefabricated container. Or, build your own unit cheaply with used materials in the following way:

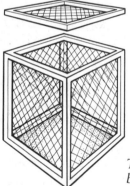

Two examples of homemade compost bins: (left) This single bin is particularly useful for the preparation of leaf mould. (right) The double bin has holes drilled in the sides to allow air to circulate.

IF SPACE IS A PROBLEM • For balconies and small city gardens: poke a bunch of small holes in the sides of a plastic garbage can and keep your kitchen wastes and plant clippings in there. Roll it around occasionally to keep the material inside suitably mingled and aerated. A 30-gallon

(120 litre) plastic garbage container with firm-locking lid and wheels will be even easier to move into place.

IF SPACE ISN'T A PROBLEM • Install two bins: one for holding material and the other in which to build the actual compost pile.

• Have a compost bin for kitchen wastes (plus clippings, and the formula below) and another larger one for leaves and garden detritus. Stockpile and keep adding layer by layer.

I have one small section of the garden where I throw all sorts of biggish stuff like woody stems, chunky plants, extra leaves. I chop them up as much as I can and twice a year turn the pile over. I don't expect much action out of this for a couple of years. In another area (again it doesn't take more than a few square feet (metres) of space), I layer chopped up leaves with manure and can usually spread it around in a few months. Then I have the Soilsaver in which I layer kitchen waste with garden detritus. I usually get very rough stuff out of there in a matter of weeks.

To make the layering easier, I have a garbage container beside the composter. I put chopped up garden discards in it and use this to cover kitchen scraps. I turn the pile every five days and attempt to be fairly scrupulous about what's in each layer.

There's a double unit that will be introduced to the garden as soon as space can be cleared for it. As far as I'm concerned, you can't have too many compost piles especially if the garden has lots of trees and shrubs. I get an average of twenty large bags of leaves and I recycle every one plus any that I can nab from the street when neighbors throw them out.

There is another quite interesting composter now available (and a Canadian invention at that). It's called the Green Cone. It has an open basket bottom which is put into a

20-inch (50 centimetre) hole. The cone is placed on top and tightly sealed—this keeps animals out. In this you can dump everything including meat and fish bones and things that don't break down in an ordinary composter (eggshells, for example, which seem to last a millennium). Water is drawn out of the waste by the earth around it reducing about 70 to 90 percent of the matter. The rest gradually disappears. It's cleared out once a year.

STUFF FOR THE COMPOST

You need about a cubic yard (metre) of material to begin a compost heap. If you don't have this much, go straight to vermicomposting (see page 31). To get started, it is possible to buy commercial activators, compost accelerators they are usually called. Save your money. They aren't necessary if you have a good mix to compost. The most important thing to remember is to have a great diversity of material in order to provide the most nutrients for plants: some completed compost, good garden soil, a sprinkling of blood meal or chopped up nettles will perform as activators. The finer the grind of everything in the heap, the faster the rotting process. Put the following in the compost:

- grass clippings that haven't been poisoned with herbicides;
- chopped up leaves. If you have space for an acid compost, use oak and beech but they will take much longer to break down;
- anything from the garden such as weeds (no seeds please), stems chopped up; tomato and squash vines;
- sawdust, ground up wood chips and nutshells, coffee grounds, dried blood meal;
- kitchen wastes, cut up fine or run through a food processor with a little water (this is a good way to add moisture to the heap);

24

- manure;
- peat moss—this won't add any nutrients to the heap but will lighten the texture;
- leaf mould;
- ashes from the fireplace;
- feathers;
- lint from the dryer;
- corn cobs are really tough to break down so cut them up;
- poultry and bird cage litter;
- shredded paper (no glossy or waxed surfaces);
- hair—your own or your pet's;
- newspapers shredded up—they are cellulose-based. Use the black and white section only unless you're sure the paper uses vegetable-based inks.

STUFF TO AVOID IN THE COMPOST

- meat, bones, cheese and all other dairy products;
- anything from the barbecue;
- cat and dog feces—too tricky. There was a salmonella outbreak in British Columbia traced to vegetables grown in compost that contained cat feces;
- absolutely any garden clippings or plants that have had pesticides, herbicides, or any other toxic chemicals sprayed on them.
- anything sick or blighted;
- anything that isn't biodegradable.

LAYERING THE COMPOST PILE

When I first composted I just made a pile and tossed stuff on it until it seemed big enough. Then I left it alone until it was ready to use—in a year or so—and moved on to another area. Once I started making layers of different kinds of material, things speeded up dramatically. It took a while before I learned that I needed to have some sort of container; that all the stuff from the garden should be cut up as small as possible; and that it needed to be dampened down slightly. Slow learner, I guess; it certainly wasn't lack of interest but then I had enough piles to always have some compost ready to spread around.

About this business of cutting everything up in tiny pieces—the street compost companions, Amanda, Laurie and I, went together and bought a chipper/shredder a few years ago. We geared ourselves up in the recommended goggles, leather gloves, huge earmuff-style protectors—this should tell you something about the noise. It was incredible. Terrifying. Sure we got good stuff but what we did to the air about us suddenly didn't seem worth it.

How often do we use it? Well, that was it—once. It was a hideously expensive experiment and the ridiculous thing didn't even chop up leaves. Yet my friend Tim bought a really expensive, heavy-duty chipper/shredder and he swears by it. If you are going to buy one, get a large enough group together to go for the big one and make it a community effort. I've heard of using a Whipper Snipper in a plastic garbage container to chop up leaves. But that is another screaming electric machine. Some people pile up leaves and run an electric lawn mower over them. Make sure there's something containing the leaves or you'll have shreds all over the place.

Me? I'm making do with heavy clippers to cut up the outside stuff and a food processor to chop up the inside stuff. Noise and air pollution also have to be considered as well as the benefits of what you're putting into the soil.

HOW TO LAYER

To make compost you need air, heat and moisture. Make your pile between four feet (1 metre) and six feet (1½ metres) high. An effective compost must have layers of different materials. Just throwing in all your kitchen wastes or all leaves will not work quickly and will end up smelling terrible because of anaerobic action. The parasites, pests, seeds and diseases are burned off in the heating process. By having it properly aired, you'll also help eliminate any smells. During the process of composting, carbon dioxide is given off (it's odorless) and nitrogen stays about the same if the pile is balanced.

Make the first layer of relatively large chunky material such as twiggy clippings to aerate the bottom. I always build mine straight on the soil so that worms and microbes can find their way into the pile as quickly as possible. I lose a few nutrients this way but not enough to be a worry.

Think green and brown, and make each layer about 6 inches (15 centimetres) thick—but remember this doesn't have to be rigid. It should be fun—not painful measuring.
- **Green stuff:** kitchen stuff, grass clippings, plant detritus.
- **Brown stuff:** manure, soil, blood meal.

Moisten the lot and turn it in a few days to mix it up. Have something to aerate the pile, something you can wiggle around in the middle to make sure it's heating up uniformly. Any kind of tube or metal pipe will work. If the pile seems a bit slow to heat up, speed things up with a sprinkling of blood meal, a hoof and horn meal mixture, or manure. Or pour manure tea over the top (manure that's been sitting in a bucket of water for a week).

HOT ROT

To use this method you must think beyond mere layering to the *nitrogen:carbon* ratio. You want the pile to hit a high of 160°F (70°C) to kill off any insect eggs, larvae, weed seeds, diseases—all the things you don't want to spread around the garden. Basic components of the pile are:

Nitrogen: the most important ingredient in the compost pile—without nitrogen things get off to a very slow start indeed. High nitrogen content in manure, urine and grass acts to heat up the pile. Chicken manure is especially high in nitrogen, as well as blood meal, tea leaves, peanut shells, bone meal, urine (human or animal, diluted three times—how you get this is your problem, just use your imagination), feathers, wool wastes, green plants and grass clippings.

Potassium: wood and plant ash (added when the compost is turned—put it on too soon and nitrogen is lost), water lily stems, urine (human or animal diluted three times), oak leaves, banana peels, fruit tree leaves.

Phosphorus: rock phosphate, bone meal, marine products, sewage sludge, blood meal, wool wastes, plant ash. These materials will conserve the nitrogen in the pile.

Trace minerals: rock dusts, marine products, sewage.

Carbon: old leaves, hay, sawdust, dried grass, weeds, paper and straw. These should all be slightly damp when added to the pile. Carbon is lost as carbon dioxide but the nitrogen should stay at the same level.

Recommended ratio: you can find anything from a ratio of 14 to 40 of carbon to each part nitrogenous material. Soil expert Dr. Stuart B. Hill says the carbon/nitrogen ratio should be from 35:1 to 30:1 carbon:nitrogen.

How do you know if you haven't got this ratio? The pile won't heat up.

If you compost in a container, it's easy to mix by eye. Kitchen wastes can be allowed to accumulate in a garbage pail until you're ready to put them in the compost.

It's an ad hoc learning experience and you should end up composting almost by instinct. If the pile doesn't heat up, but is wet enough, you haven't got enough nitrogen. The easiest remedy is to sprinkle some blood meal on top. If you've got too much nitrogen, then it'll smell like ammonia.

When my pile doesn't smell right (soft, earthy), I just throw some soil on top and this seems to right things almost immediately. It's also a good way to top off the pile. A day or so later, the pile will heat up and continue heating up for a couple of weeks. Then, turn the whole heap over.

Turning the pile is made much easier if you have two bins and all you have to do is move decaying stuff from one to the other. If not, you'll have to work in your own small space. Turning blends the pile as well as aerating it.

Here's the 14-day method recommended in the *Rodale Encyclopedia of Organic Gardening*:
1. Shred everything going into the pile. Mix after shredding and put into a pile not more than 5 feet (150 centimetres) high.
2. Moisten material evenly without making it soggy.
3. Leave for three days. Then turn every two or three days. Use it after a few weeks.
With the 14-day method, you lose fewer nutrients. After a few weeks, it won't be perfect but you can use it around the garden as the decaying process continues.

COMPOST AND CHEMICALS • The question most often asked of composting experts is what about all those chemicals applied to our food? How will this affect the compost?

What about composting kitchen waste that hasn't been organically grown? By using a brown/green mixture in the compost, you will reduce the damage because of the heat generated. But there are four hundred pesticides registered for use on food crops in the US and a great deal of our food is imported from there. Some of these pesticides can remain in the soil for years without breaking down. If you're worried and put a lot of potato or fruit peels in your compost, by all means have it tested. In tests some poisons such as 2-4-D just didn't go away, and about 74 percent remained even after a year of composting; with others such as the insecticide lindane, anywhere from 55 percent to 99 percent remained in the compost.

It might be time to switch to organically grown food if it's available. Obviously if you are growing your own, you won't have to worry about this problem. I belong to a food co-operative and that's part of our business—searching out farmers and suppliers who grow non-chemically. Organically grown food tastes a lot better than most supermarket stuff anyway. Read the *Organic* label carefully. The symbol of the Canadian Organic Growers is a horn of plenty. One of their standards is: only soil that has not been treated chemically for at least five years. Given the half-life of most pesticides this is an absolute must. There are a thousand certified growers in Canada. Look for them.

EARTHWORM TEA • You can make formidable compost by raising earthworms in a trash can. Earthworm castings are incredibly rich in nutrients.
- Take an uncovered 21-gallon (95-litre) plastic trash can, insert a plastic spigot about six inches (15 centimetres) from the bottom.
- Fill the can with a mix of grass clippings, leaves and partially decayed fruit or vegetable scraps.

- Add enough water so the worms can live comfortably in decaying vegetable matter above the water line. Worms produce nutrient-rich castings as they digest the organic matter.
- Wash water down over the compost and castings and extract from the bottom. Add the same amount of water to the can that you draw off. Plug up the plastic spigot.

By adding more water you drive the worms and other useful chewing insects back to the top. And the cycle begins again.

WORM COMPOSTING • Vermicomposting is ideal for those of us who live in the north, or in apartments and want to continue to recycle household wastes all winter. Use redworms, which are thinner than earthworms. They eat their own weight in organic matter daily, and you'll get finished stuff in two to three months.

- Keep the container indoors during the winter so that you can keep composting all year long. You do not want your worms to freeze. Since they are odorless and won't squirm all over your floors—they hate being exposed to the light—you don't run any risk in this venture.
- Use a box (wood or plastic) with a lid. The worms need a dark moist place to live in.
- Bedding material: straw, peat moss, manure, leaves, newsprint (again shredded and without colored ink that might be contaminated), cardboard, grass clippings. You can bury kitchen detritus in this muck.
- Take redworms from your compost or order them (see page 36).
- When castings (the dark stuff) are complete, move to one side and make a new bed—they'll migrate to the new area.

In her book *Worms Eat My Garbage*, Mary Appelhof recommends a container 1 foot (30 centimetres) deep, 2 feet (60 centimetres) wide, and 3 feet (90 centimetres) long. Put a bottom on if it's to be used indoors and no bottom if only outside. Make sure there are holes for air.

The Rodale encyclopedia recommends a box 2 feet (60 centimetres) to 3 feet (90 centimetres) square, and 2 feet (60 centimetres) high. Use a mix of weeds, leaves, grass clippings, 15 percent manure, 12 percent topsoil; kitchen garbage can substitute for manure. Mix thoroughly and put in box. Buy redworms; if the mix is too hot, add water before adding worms. Keep watered but not soggy. For the best compost, you want a good combination of worms, bacteria and fungi.

COLD WEATHER COMPOST • You can make this in fall and allow it to overwinter. The heap will be ready by spring. Pile size is the key because extreme cold or excessive moisture slow it down—the larger the pile, the better the insulation. The outermost layer of organic material will provide protection. Make it as big as 4 feet (1.2 metres) high, 7 feet (2 metres) wide, and 14 feet (4.2 metres) long, or as small as 4 feet (1.2 metres) by 6 (1.8 metres) by 7 (2 metres). If you start it smack in the middle of the garden, it will feed the soil below. Covering it with black plastic will speed things along. This method can work to −5°F (−20°C). The outer layers freeze, but thaw quickly.

Make separate piles of material—garden waste, leaves, straw, manure—and let them get dampened by fall rain. Then spread the stuff out to dry. Try a straw-manure mix. Alternate 1-inch (2.5-centimetre) layers; any unshredded garden waste will provide air pockets. Make into long flat rectangle. Three weeks later, once the pile has cooled down, turn and mix the wet areas with dry to break up any clumps. At this stage, minimize the surface and make a rounded mound as tall as possible. Let sit until needed in spring. Scatter worms throughout pile. They'll keep on digesting all winter. Raw materials shrink by about 50 percent leaving 15 cubic yards (11 cubic metres) of winter compost.

SIMPLE WINTER COMPOSTING • I put spare leaves into plastic bags, dampen them slightly and add a little soil and manure. I leave them piled up and occasionally toss them around. By spring they are in good enough shape to be used as leaf mould (see *Mulch* page 42).

For regular compost, save a bag or so of leaves, keep some dirt from freezing in a garage or shed. Carry on putting kitchen wastes in your bin, add the leaves and soil when you think it's necessary. In spring this stuff will really compost quickly. It won't be using much oxygen but you'll be supplying nitrogen from the food, and carbon from the leaves.

ACID COMPOST • This can be useful if you are bumping up the acidity in sections of the garden. Chop up oak leaves and stuff them into a garbage bag, slightly dampened. Add soil and manure and roll the bag around to mix. Use it in spring around acid-loving plants.

My Auntie Marge does the following: she keeps all her fruit and vegetable peelings, tea bags and so on in a small plastic bag at the side of the sink. As soon as the bag is full, she puts water in it, ties the ends together, puts it in a nice shady spot under a tree, and then makes a slit down the middle. Everything inside gradually rots and there's no smell at all. Worms get inside and do their work. She piles lawn clippings and other garden rubbish on top of the bags—just so no one complains. In February (she lives on the west coast), she digs a trench, fills it with the contents of a few bags and plants her peas.

Another word about dog and cat feces—don't, as some advise, put them in the compost. The protein in the food waste may attract animals, and they may have parasites that won't do anyone any good. There is a thing called Doggie Dooley: it's a plastic garbage can with holes in the side that you sink into the ground. Active enzymes are added to break down the feces. Do-it-yourself: in a well-drained place but not near tree roots, dig a hole 1½ feet (.5 metres) deep, 12 inches (30 centimetres) wide, put in a plastic bucket with holes punched near the top and a secure lid. Tuck stones or gravel down the outside. Put in the dog or cat droppings, add half a box of septic starter and a litre of water. Wait a couple of days, then add feces every day. Pour in a bucket of water once a week, a packet of septic starter once or twice a month. The liquid created oozes through the holes near the rim (from *The Vancouver Sun*).

EXTRA TREATS FOR THE COMPOST

- Comfrey grows fast and spreads like crazy. Keep chopping it back to contain it and put the bits into the compost. It adds as much to the C:N ratio as manure.
- Stinging nettle contains iron, speeds up decay.
- Yarrow or *Achillea* has properties that add trace elements to the compost.
- All those sow bugs you see in the compost aren't yucky—they are very effectively breaking up the decaying matter. The diversity of animal life in the compost should be enormous.

COMPOST PROBLEMS

- If you see flies buzzing around, add a layer of soil and be sure to bury fruit and kitchen material.

- If the stack is too wet, it's going to smell awful especially on a warm summer's day. It means you've got to get some air in there. Turn the pile, add something absorbent like a little soil or peat.
- It will also smell if you haven't got a good enough mix. Too much of any one element just doesn't work properly. Keep the green-brown layers in mind.
- If it's too dry, it may mean the heap is just too big. You'll probably have to resort the layers and dampen them down.
- If it isn't heating up, it means you need nitrogen. Here's the nitrogen list again: blood meal, kitchen scraps, *fresh* manure (not an easy commodity to find in the middle of the city but I include it in case you have access to a farm), fresh grass clippings that have not been treated with a herbicide.
- If the pile is only warm and moist in the middle, it's probably too small. Add more well-moistened material.

Rotten egg odor: Pile is anaerobic—not enough air, turn it daily for a few days.

Ammonia odor: Too much nitrogen—add carbon (straw, sawdust, leaves, newspapers); then turn to let gas escape.

COMPOST TEA • This is a surprisingly effective way to make a little compost go a long way. Just pour water over a porous bag filled with compost and leave it for a week in a large container. Dilute it by half with more water if it seems to be getting very strong. You can even add some manure. Quite often I just put a shovel full of compost in a pail, fill it with hot water and swish it around. When it cools off, it's ready to use.

FINISHED COMPOST • Well-prepared, finished compost has a crumbly texture like humus. If it hasn't, put it through a coarse sieve and toss the unfinished material back into the compost for another go. It should be quite dark and have a pleasant smell.

HOW TO USE COMPOST

• Compost, like any soil amender, can be dug into the earth, or used as top or side dressing around a plant. What it does:
• Loosens up clay soil; retains water in sand; adds all essential nutrients.
• It's classified as a soil conditioner rather than a fertilizer but provides trace elements on a time-release basis better than anything else does.
• Use it everywhere including as part of a seed-starting mix.

• • •

You can be as casual or as complicated as you want about your composting—just don't throw out material that can be returned to the earth. But don't get trapped into competitive composting. It is such a pain to go to a party and hear people trying to one-up each other about the quality of their compost. This is supposed to be good for *you* as well as your garden.

Resources
Redworms can be bought from:
Early Bird Bait and Ecology Farms
R.R. #1
Smithville, Ont. L0R 2A0
416-643-4251

The Worm Farm
31 Herman Avenue
Toronto, Ont.
M6R 1Y1
416-588-5280

CHAPTER THREE

MULCHING AND FERTILIZING: TO FEED AND PROTECT

WHY MULCH?

MULCHING SEEMS TO BE A BAFFLING GARDEN SUB-ject. A lot of people don't bother. But think of the soil with the same kind of tenderness you do your own skin. Almost automatically you protect it from sun, wind and lashing rain. Soil needs exactly the same treatment. Mulching is the answer. It means covering the earth to protect it from crippling damage by the sun, keeping it moisturized, and preventing weeds from growing in the wrong place. In winter, plants are cossetted by mulch, which also feeds the soil as it breaks down.

Sounds like a magic hit? There's more. It will save you a ton of work. Weeding is reduced to practically nothing when you mulch. You won't disturb tender root systems by cultivating because mulching eliminates that chore. Temperatures are kept moderate because mulch cools the soil during the day and warms it at night.

There's even more. A good mulch will help feed the ever-valuable earthworms as it adds a wide spectrum of nutrients to the soil during decomposition. It helps to keep the soil from becoming compacted and thereby messing up the lives of bacteria and other good organisms.

In the forest, whatever falls to the ground eventually disintegrates to become humus. This rich black organic material is the lifeline of the natural world. What we do with mulching serves much the same function. Even when there is a drought, a layer of mulch will continue to provide food for the soil and keep it relatively cool and moist. Any kind of mulch will help to reduce the amount of watering you need to do, because it cuts down on evaporation and holds moisture in the ground where it's needed.

There has to be a downside to all this of course. It can become home to slugs, earwigs and other little beasts. But you can easily shove the mulch to one side, pick out the offending little creatures, then cover up again. I tend not to worry about what's going on under there. Think of mulch as a way to trap pests and it improves your attitude immeasurably.

But the final argument for mulching is that it will probably keep diseases at bay. According to Dr. Stuart Hill, microbial toxins released during mulch decomposition help control disease; and certain nematode-destroying fungi are encouraged by soil conditions under the mulch.

Commercially bagged mulch is available but it's expensive. It's easy to make your own and you can be confident about exactly what you are putting on the soil and near your plants.

HOW TO MULCH

It's important to mulch twice a year—in spring through the growing season; and then again *after* the ground has frozen. You can mulch once plants are established as long as you don't let it touch any new growth of the stems. This is generally a good practice—you don't want to cut off oxygen to the plants or set up any conditions whereby new plant material can easily rot. Another good idea is to use a thin layer of finely shredded material rather than a whole lot of loose unshredded stuff in mulch.

GENERAL MULCHING PRACTICES
- First prepare the soil, plant as usual, level with a rake— then apply the mulch to evenly raked soil.
- Add manure, leaf mould, compost to top layer of soil.
- Plants that need a deep mulch for winter protection should have a mulch layer 3 inches (7.5 centimetres) deep put on once frost persists during the day. Mulch tends to moderate temperatures, keeping them even, and this action will help avoid the ravages of freeze-thaw cycles which can rip plants right out of the ground. Remove it in spring and toss it straight into the compost where it will continue to break down. Then reapply as needed during the summer.

MULCHING PROBLEMS
- I've talked to people who are afraid to mulch because they've managed to kill off plants by doing so. It usually turns out that they put mulch on when the ground was too soggy or too dry. This is especially dangerous when you've got young transplants. Don't mulch until the plants show new growth.

There are a few more things you should be wary of:
- Don't let mulch touch the base of any plant.
- Never mulch on water-logged soils—air won't be able to get at the soil. You also run the risk of developing mould.
- Never mulch on dead dry soils—it will draw out whatever small amount of moisture there is in the soil.

WHAT TO USE AS MULCH
Here is a partial list of material you can use for mulch:

- Leaves: Just about the best thing you can use. Shred them as finely as possible or use unshredded ones mixed with straw.
- Evergreen boughs, pine needles: beg, borrow or steal as much as you can. They will also protect small shrubs from fierce winter winds. They are especially welcomed by acid-loving plants.
- Grass clippings untouched by herbicides; you can leave them on your lawn as they are — this is still mulching. But you can also clear them off once or twice a year to use as a speeding activator in your compost pile if it shows signs of turning cold.
- Pine cones — these look great and allow moisture to get through. But they are a pain in the neck if you have great piles of leaves landing on them — it's impossible to rake them off. They are most effective under large shrubs and away from trees such as maples.
- Straw and hay are excellent protection against the drying winter winds. Spread layers several inches (centimetres) thick over empty beds. When you're ready to plant, pull the material aside and proceed as usual. Make sure neither contains any seeds. Add compost to the soil before using these as mulches.
- Coffee grounds and tea leaves can be recycled as mulches especially around acid plants.
- Newspaper shredded up is quite effective. The ink no longer contains lead; even color sections are printed with clay-based inks; however, avoid the glossy magazine sections.
- Marble chips.
- Photodegradable film.
- Cocoa bean hulls can absorb more than twice their weight in water and look good as a side benefit.
- Mixed tree trimmings shredded as fine as possible.
- Seaweed.

- Composted rice hulls, buckwheat hulls.
- Shells from the following nuts: almonds, pecans, ground up hazelnuts, peanuts.
- Stones.
- Weeds and anything else from the vegetable garden cut up as long as you've made sure there are no seeds. If this doesn't suit you aesthetically, put a layer of cocoa hulls, or something similar, on top. I prefer to put them in the compost, but this is terrific if you're short of mulching material.
- Corn cobs ground up in 1-inch (2.5-centimetre) pieces but must have blood meal, cottonseed meal, bone meal or compost underneath.
- Peat moss must be well-moistened: pour hot water over and let it sit before use. Because it doesn't add any nutrients, add manure and some compost.
- Salt hay grows in the marshy lands near the sea. It is excellent if you are lucky enough to have access to such an area.
- Sawdust: add soybean meal, cottonseed meal or compost to the soil before mulching.
- Cedar bark, wood chips and wood wastes if they are chopped up finely enough look good and allow moisture to seep through successfully.
- Discarded fabrics such as old rags, wool or cotton castoffs.
- Shredded unbleached paper such as the kind now being used in coffee filters.
- Black plastic is often recommended and though it does have many uses, I'm not crazy about anything that requires a lot of processing energy or is synthetic. Besides it adds nothing to the soil.

HOW TO USE COMPOST AS MULCH

- If you have very fine compost, you can apply it to the soil before you plant. The closer to planting time, the finer the grind. To get this, push the compost through a sieve and then throw the remainder back into the heap.
- Use whatever is left in the compost bin around plants in the fall once the ground is frozen. Don't worry if it looks a little raw. It will continue to decompose. Keep it away from the crown of any plant.
- Mix compost and soil and use as a side dressing. It won't burn the plants. Do this a couple of times a year.
- Compost can even be used around acid-loving plants. But if you have lots of them, make an acid compost by adding sulphur (See also *Composting* page 19).
- For plants in pots, mix one part compost with two parts soil and run it through a screen. Add 1 inch (2.5 centimetres) deep to the top.

LEAVES AS MULCH • Never, ever throw out leaves even if your area has a public composting plan. The smallest garden will probably have a corner to store leaves while they break down into leaf mould. In the long run, leaves are more valuable to your garden than manure—and a lot cheaper. They combine carbon dioxide, minerals, nitrogen, phosphorus, calcium, magnesium and water to make food for next year's plant growth. As leaves break down, humus is produced improving the soil and making it more moisture-retentive.

Shred leaves to help them break down into their components more quickly. Dried leaves can be raked over perennial beds for winter protection. Be cautious here. Some leaves such as maple will form a thick mat once they are wet. This can smother plants, undoing whatever good mulch is supposed to provide. In spring rake them off and put them into the compost or other piles to further break down.

One section of my garden is specially for leaves. I dig a hole, put down layers of leaves, dampen slightly, then a layer of manure combined with soil. This provides the medium through which nitrogen can start the process of decay. I keep doing this until there's a reasonable pile. It's never reasonable enough because I always have bags of leaves left over. It's topped off with a layer of soil. This breaks down slowly to be distributed around the garden the following year. Leaf mould such as this will hold up to ten times the moisture of regular soil.

I bag up the leftover leaves (and anyone else's I can snag), make them moist but not soggy, add some manure and soil. By spring it's astonishing how much this has decomposed. My composting companion, Amanda, also collects leaves that others put out. She piles bags full of them over her pond to form a layer of protection for her fish. In spring the leaves go into the compost or, if they've broken down enough, are dug into new beds.

Leaves taught me a great lesson years ago. One area of the garden was turned into part of a basketball court for the kids. Once they left home, I had the surface removed and found not a worm in what looked like dead soil. For a few years I threw all the leaves from the garden into that area. Then I started turning it over, adding manure and now I've worms and plants flourishing there.

- A layer of leaves in the compost is essential for the heap's health.
- Make an acid mulch for your rhododendrons and other acid-loving plants with oak leaves or pine needles.
- Be sure to rake maple leaves off lawns and beds since they tend to form a mat once they are wet. Let them break down into leaf mould first.

PEAT MOSS AS MULCH • Once again we're in an area of controversy. Bogs are home to wildlife. As we strip these bogs of peat, we're also slowly eroding our wetlands.

According to *Harrowsmith* magazine, bog covers 425,000 square miles (1 million square kilometres)—about 12 percent of our total land mass. Of this, 10 percent to 20 percent is useable. Canadian peat bogs have been forming for more than 10,000 years and some of them are now 20 to 30 feet (6 to 9 metres) deep. It takes about 300 years to create a foot (30 centimetres) of peat moss. Again you have to consult your conscience about continuing to use peat.

- Sphagnum moss has a low pH.
- Always dampen before mixing; never let peat moss dry out. Peat moss must be soaked for a week so that it won't absorb moisture from the soil. To dampen, slit bag, put slow running hose over slit or leave out in rain. What it does best is provide some protection for the soil. I like to combine it with other elements such as manure.
- For acid loving plants: damp sphagnum peat mixed with compost made without lime or wood ashes. Don't mulch with peat alone; it will draw water from soil. Sphagnum peat can absorb huge amounts of water.
- Peat is useful to deodorize and lighten compost.
- For cuttings: use dampened peat moss blended with perlite to form a lightweight sterile medium. It will be moisture-retentive, well-aerated and quick to drain—ideal for cuttings.
- Plants grown in a blend with some good garden soil need less coddling than those in a soil-less mix.

NEWSPAPER AS MULCH • If your local newspaper uses a nontoxic ink, you can try the following:

- After you've seeded an area, wet the soil and cover the ground with dampened newspapers. Keep checking on

whether the seeds are germinating and whether they need water. Once the seedlings start to sprout, fold the paper so it acts as a mulch between plants.
- Rake it off in the spring to let the soil warm up. This can also be added to the compost to break down even further.

CREATIVE MULCHING

Your true designer mulch can make a garden look clean and tidy and give it a consistent look between lashings of color from plants and shrubs. It can be effective in keeping plants from getting splashed by heavy rains.

Designer mulch: I like to use a combination of compost, ground up leaves or leaf mould with a topping of cocoa hulls. It looks and smells like a chocolate bar for a few days (certainly throws you off eating the stuff for a while). But once it tones down and turns a pleasant greyish brown, it looks very neat.

Stone mulching: In some borders a stone mulch looks perfect. They heat up quickly in spring and keep warm at night. Cultivate the soil deeply and add lots of organic matter. Top off with a layer of stones. This is particularly good for alpine plants since it echoes the original circumstances of many of them.

Living mulches: You can create a truly aesthetic soil cover by planting a living mulch. This can be a ground cover, a spreading shrub or ornamental grasses. It will keep the soil intact, provide a floor for your garden, add color, texture and warmth. This also has the virtue of adding diversity to the garden. I've used a collection of about fifteen kinds of thyme in my front garden and it has a sensual tapestry effect.

FERTILIZING

I have never used chemical fertilizers partly because I didn't understand the NPK (nitrogen, phosphorus, potassium) stuff on the labels. Eventually I avoided them because it just didn't seem logical to pay a lot of money for fertilizers when compost could do the trick el cheapo. I didn't realize at first that the basis of all organic gardening is to "Feed the soil, not the plant." It's an aphorism worth repeating and makes great sense. Once you've got the healthiest soil possible, it is simple to keep it that way. What you do in the ecological garden is imitate nature as closely as possible. Since soil comprises minerals and humus, it seems sensible to use rock fertilizers for mineralization, and organic material that will break down into humus.

A healthy soil contains just about every element it needs: nitrogen, phosphorus and potassium; zinc, manganese, boron, iron, sulphur, copper, magnesium, molybdenum, chlorine, lots of organic matter and humus. It will be well-drained and friable.

Fertilizers are absorbed by the plant's root system. They provide the extra nutrients the plant may require. An organic fertilizer feeds as it decomposes. The rate of decomposition depends on the temperature, moisture and the pH of the soil. Fertilizers are the food for all the large and small organisms in the soil. You want to treat them as well as you treat yourself—with a balanced diet. And just like all diets, they vary.

Organic fertilizers provide the same nutrients as inorganic fertilizers. But with inorganic fertilizers, the nutrients come from sources other than living matter or ones that don't have a carbon structure. These synthetics rush to the root immediately. If you add too much, you run the risk of root burn. Since the nature of plants is still such a mystery even to trained scientists, we poor souls without that kind of background aren't necessarily going to make the perfect choices for our plants.

Your soil can be tested to see if you have any major nutrients missing but usually the condition of your plants will let you know this (See *Soil* page 8). The pH of your soil is going to influence how nutrients are absorbed.

Fertilizer is any material that gives the plant nutrients for development and growth. Organic material is matter that will break down, decay and, in the process, feed the soil.

- A complete fertilizer contains nitrogen, phosphorus and potassium.
- An incomplete fertilizer has only one or two of these elements.
- To understand fertilizer analysis, you must know that 20-10-5, for example, means there is 20 percent nitrogen, 10 percent phosphorus, 5 percent potassium. It's all relative—20-10-5 contains four times as much nitrogen as potassium, twice as much phosphorus, that is, a ratio of 4-2-1.
- All living matter, plant or animal, is composed of compounds with carbon structure. Proteins, fats, carbohydrates and other compounds synthesized by an organism have one common factor, a carbon structure. Truly organic fertilizers must consist of nutrient elements derived from compounds with a carbon structure. Any of these is an organic fertilizer when placed in the soil—manure, bone meal and chopped garden detritus. These will provide a slow-release, non-burning source of nutrition. The effect will stay in the soil rather than leach out. Anything organic will eventually provide the wonder of wonders—humus which will, in turn, improve any soil.
- Rock fertilizers: at least we have a lot of this stuff since that's what the earth is made of. They provide trace elements to the soil as they break down slowly. You

should apply them with organic matter since they do not supply any nitrogen. They last from five to ten years.

—Phosphate rock: source of phosphorus and trace elements including zinc, boron, iodine, iron oxide, iron sulphide, calcium fluoride, calcium carbonate, manganese dioxide. It's not soluble in water but it stays put in the soil so it's always available for use when the roots finally reach it. Superphosphate is treated with sulphuric acid. This makes it more soluble and more expensive because it uses so much energy in production. It's easy, of course, and that makes it very tempting. It can cause imbalances in soil microbes and a buildup of salts. I used it with great abandon until I found this out. Back to basics—granite dust is an excellent source of potash. It has trace elements and is a lot cheaper than chemical potash fertilizers. It won't change the pH and is slow to release potash. You can use it as a top dressing.

—Potash rock contains potassium plus a wide variety of trace minerals. Apply with organic material straight into the soil or the compost heap.

THE CHEMICALS • Be wary of the company that will inevitably come around to fertilize your property (for lots of money) with synthetic "organic" fertilizers. More chemicals.

Chemical fertilizers are the magic bullets that really only serve to give an instant boost. It's the long-term effects you must be wary about. These fertilizers destroy all the important living creatures in the soil, especially earthworms. The soil itself becomes less friable. Chemicals prevent some plants from absorbing nutrients. And, of course, since these chemicals are water-soluble, they will eventually leach into the ground water, muck up our streams, rivers and lakes. Some of the chemicals zip through the soil like the proverbial dose of salts. They go so swiftly that they don't pause long enough to help out the plants. Others accumulate in the soil and really mess things up. If they become concentrated, they can react with clay to form a hardpan—through which no water can move. You can't count on the chemical reaction that a synthetic will have with your particular soil. Your plants depend on a balanced supply of nutrients. And it's this balance that is so important. Plants can't screen out ionized chemicals and they are in danger of becoming saturated with unbalanced materials.

The side-effects can destroy the fertility of your soil because they kill off beneficial organisms. The natural world is very complicated and we simply haven't enough information about it. Once we start tampering, we're just as apt to mess things up. Apart from all the other dangers, chemical fertilizers are expensive. Go simple, go natural.

As I've said before, earthworms are our friends. Without them, the soil becomes infertile. They can clean up a garden by ingesting 90 percent of the leaves that fall. But they are delicate organisms. Imagine how a worm feels when it's hit with a dose of chemicals. It does what you'd expect if you think about it for a minute. It dies. If not, the chemicals can concentrate in their bodies and kill off the birds that eat them.

What is lethal to them are copper compounds, chloropicrin, methane, sodium methyl bromide; DDT; chlordane. Read the labels of anything you intend to put into your garden. Some other inorganics: ammonium nitrate, ammonium phosphate, potassium nitrate, and potassium chloride. These *may* provide nutrient salts immediately which a plant may need. But don't count on them helping out your soil over the long term.

ABOUT NITROGEN FERTILIZERS • You're going to hear about how organic this or that fertilizer is because it's made of nitrogen. What could be more organic? Nitrogen is in the air—in fact about 78 percent of the atmosphere is made of gaseous nitrogen. It's free, of course, but during the processing a great deal is lost and a huge amount of energy is required.

Healthy soil has enough nitrogen-fixing bacteria for any plant's requirement. These antibiotic-producing bacteria keep plant disease under control.

- By using synthetics, you can end up making your plants much more vulnerable to disease. High nitrogen fertilizers can kill off some of the natural nitrogen-fixing bacteria. With soluble nitrates, these bacteria then become dependent on artificial nitrogen. Once you start that, how do you stop?
- Nitrates can build up in both water and in plant tissues. Research from the Massachusetts Institute of Technology shows that bacteria convert nitrates to nitrites. These become the raw material for nitrosamines which can cause cancer in animals.
- Runoff of nitrates in ponds and streams can cause a buildup of algae and other aquatic vegetation. They use up the oxygen supply in the water. Then the living creatures in the water are bumped off.

OTHER STUFF TO AVOID • **Potassium nitrate**: 39 percent potash, 13 percent nitrogen. It separates the clay particles and long-term use will ruin the soil by destroying its porosity. **Potassium sulphate**: 48 percent potash, 16 percent sulphur in the form of gypsum.

Many of the chemicals used in pesticides were developed for chemical warfare. Stuff like malathion and diazinon (lethal to honeybees) freezes nerves and muscles. If you use any of these, you have to wear protective clothing. Parathion can be absorbed by the skin. These chemicals can kill just about anything else as well as what they're supposed to be hitting. These organic phosphate insecticides do, however, break down into nontoxics sooner than other chemicals.

THE ORGANICS

The most efficient way to fertilize is to imitate nature. Soil originally came from rock. Since soils and plants evolved at the same time, using the minerals from rocks will feed them when they need the nutrients. The warmer and more moist the atmosphere, the faster nutrients will become available to the plants and the better they'll grow. And there's no problem with an excess supply that might harm the plant.

ROCK FERTILIZERS • Many organic producers swear by rock powders and when you read about the extraordinary results produced by them you realize they are among the best of organic fertilizers. Any kind of organic matter is going to improve your soil's capacity to retain water. They will also keep nitrogen in the soil and make nutrients available to plants.

MANURES • **Worm castings** are among the most gorgeous looking and best stuff to use on your soil. They are richer in calcium, potassium and phosphorus than any other organic product.

I use composted **sheep manure**, which has a higher nitrogen content than cow manure—sheep digest more efficiently than cows. Some organic gardeners, however, don't like the idea of using any kind of animal by-products though this hasn't bothered me so far. But I'm moving in that direction since I seldom eat meat and we now know that the gases produced by cows burping are adding to the greenhouse effect.

There is a never-ending supply of animal manure: one cow will produce 27,000 pounds (12,250 kilograms), of which only about a third is returned to the soil without being damaged. Manure contains a high content of bacteria.

Cold manure: has a high water content and ferments slowly—cow, hog manure.

Hot manure: richer in nitrogen, more easily fermented: sheep, poultry, horse.

The *Encyclopedia of Organic Gardening* stresses that it's pointless making comparisons between the NKP of synthetic fertilizers and manure. Manure is far more valuable: it provides trace elements not found in the synthetics, as well as organic matter necessary to the life of the soil. That turns into humus. Humus makes nutrients available to plants.

Fresh manure should be well-enough composted that any weed seeds have been destroyed.

When to apply manure:
Spring: as you prepare your beds. You can apply it to sod before a light rain but not when you're expecting a heavy rain.
Summer: side dressing near plants; dig in when you are planting.
Fall: after you've cleaned up the garden when you dig in compost or peat, preparing beds for winter.
Winter: Add manure to the extra leaves in plastic bags. Add a bit of soil and moisten. Tie. In spring you'll have excellent compost; store properly in a work shed.

MANURE TEAS • My hortguru Juliet makes what she calls Eau de Chickshit, which she swears by. Like other eaux de vie, it must sit and ferment properly. Put chicken manure in a bucket of water. Strain and put the solid wastes into the compost and the liquid into a bottle. Measure about five inches (12.5 centimetres) from the edges of the lateral branches of the plant, and make a little channel with a trowel. Add the liquid to the channel. Tomatoes love this treatment. So does just about everything else.

FISH EMULSION FERTILIZER • Make your own fish emulsion: put fish scraps in a large container and add water. Cover top with wire screening to keep out animals and insects; put in an isolated location to ferment 8 to 12 weeks. This stuff can get pretty high—add citrus oil or scent to mask some of the odor. When it's finished, a layer of mineral-rich oil will float on top of the water, and the fish scales will have sunk to bottom. Skim off the oil and store in a special container. Dilute one cup (250 millilitres) in 5 gallons (22 litres) of water. It's rich in nitrogen, phosphorus and trace elements, but low in calcium.

OTHER ORGANICS • Dried blood is 10 percent to 12 percent nitrogen. Steamed bone meal is 1 percent to 3 percent nitrogen, 10 percent to 15 percent phosphorus. Raw bone meal is richer in nitrogen, 3 percent to 6 percent than steamed, but it's slower to decompose.

Hoof and horn meal is 10 percent to 16 percent nitrogen, and about 2 percent phosphorus.

If you have meat scraps and fat, treat same as fish scrap: bury deeply to keep out of the way of animals but within reach of mature plant roots.

FOLIAR FEEDING • If your soil hasn't had time to build up enough organic matter, you may need to do some short-term foliar feeding. This is feeding plants through their leaves by spraying. Use it if there's been a heat wave or you haven't been able to water regularly. ·

Spray in the morning when the plants are getting revved up for activity and it's fairly calm. Use when plants are flowering or setting fruit. Use a kelp-based product derived from marine plants. Norwegian kelp has 70 percent micro-nutrients and stimulates plant growth. It comes as a con-centrate (powder or liquid) to be mixed with water.

PRODUCTS TO LOOK FOR • Earth's Best: based on com-posted manures and natural minerals in pelletized uniform mixture, conditions soil and provides nutrients. Won't burn plants, environmentally safe.
Vermont 100 Premium Fertilizer: nontoxic blend of dried whey meal, leather and bone meal, natural nitrate of soda, sulphate of potash and cocoa shells. (Gardener's Supply Co. Dept. OG, 128 Intervale Road, Burlington, Vermont 05401, USA Tel. (802) 863-1700.

Organic Fertilizers

Product   Approximate analysis (N,P,K) by percentage

	NITRO-GEN	PHOS-PHORUS	POTASS-IUM
raw bone meal (also calcium and trace elements)	2-5	14-27	0
steamed bone meal	.7-4	18-35	0
rock phosphate	0	20-30	0
sulphate of potash magnesia	0	0	22
blood meal	12	0	0

seaweed concentrate (also plant hormones and trace elements)	1	2	3
fish emulsion	5-6	4-10	1-5

Source: *The Ecological Agriculture Projects*

CHAPTER FOUR

BUGS: THE GOOD, THE BAD AND THE MERELY UGLY

❧

I T TOOK YEARS BEFORE I ADMITTED THAT OTHER things besides plants lived in my garden. Bugs for one. I strolled through my garden quite oblivious to leaves with their edges all chewed up, foliage lacy with holes, or flower buds mysteriously lopped off. Until I saw my first slug. Maybe I was up earlier than usual. Maybe I was peering under a leaf. But there it was, slimy, oozing a sticky trail from its yucky soft body. Without hesitating, I picked it up and stepped on it. I was blooded, as they say in hunting.

I got a pair of slug-stomping slippers. I started the slug patrol and opened my eyes to all sorts of other untoward things going on in the garden. I'd heard about earwigs but never seen one until a couple of years later. Once bitten, I started after them too. Then came sow bugs, aphids— flying, crawling, creeping creatures getting smaller and smaller until I was policing the joint with a large magnifying glass.

I did not like what I saw—the more I looked the more insects there seemed to be out there. As I sat on the deck for the last breath of air before bed, I imagined a throng ready to start chewing the minute I disappeared. The sound of munching sometimes haunted my sleep. I got confused—surely these living creatures can't all be bad?

Since I didn't want to spend most of my gardening time on death-squad tactics, I decided to concentrate on the worst pests and hope that my plants would survive on their own. My job, I felt, was to design the garden properly, and feed and water the plants. They'd survive without chemical assault.

It's heartbreaking to see the evidence of our fear—no, it is hatred—of insects. Any conventional nursery shows ample evidence of this displeasure. Shelves filled with rows of skulls and crossbones, warnings to keep these products away from children and animals, and to protect yourself against toxic side effects. If you have to protect yourself so carefully, how's a poor little plant going to manage?

We're not quite sure how we got ourselves into this fix but one theory is that chemical companies had all these herbicides and chemicals stockpiled that were developed for the possibility of germ warfare. After World War II was over, there was nowhere to place them, unless the public could be convinced to buy them to get rid of everything that flew, buzzed or bit. Thus we became addicted to the quick fix.

Quel balderdash. Almost all insects, apart from those that have no effect at all, are either beneficial to us or are essential to our well-being. That leaves .1 percent (point one !) that are actually harmful. Seems hardly a fair war when you look at the man-made instruments of destruction. Although there are two to three million species of insects only .1 percent are pests for food crops and even fewer will mess up the garden. Remember that many of the .1 percent also help maintain the natural balance of life in your garden—earwigs for an obvious instance. There is an old garden saw that says "If it moves slowly enough, step on it; if it doesn't leave it—it'll probably kill something else." It's not a bad piece of advice.

To get back to pesticides for a moment—everyone should know why they are bad. One reason is that there's no such thing as a specific pesticide in spite of what you

read on the bottle. It might not be toxic for some beneficials (say bees) but be death for others (the utterly necessary earthworm). Dr. Stuart B. Hill says that the more you
use pesticides, the more you'll need to use them. "This is
because of the damage to natural controls and inevitable
development of resistance and secondary pests." Most
chemicals are incredibly inefficient. They usually miss the
target and hit something they shouldn't, such as our own
vulnerable organs, and all the beneficial organisms so important to the natural mix. Keeping that mix as diversified
as possible is also crucial to survival.

As Dr. Hill points out, there is increasing cost, decreasing
availability and dependency on something derived from
non-renewable resources. "The benefits of pesticide use
are experienced primarily by the user whereas their harmful
side-effects must be paid for by the population at large,
including the unborn populations."

If that's not a compelling enough argument, we are
acquiring more allergies because of these chemicals; and if
pesticides become wind-borne, the area they cover expands incredibly. They can hang about long after their
toxic properties are useful. Who knows how and what
beings are affected. In other words, we're losing control of
our environment when we use these chemicals. If you
believe you can control nature, there is no limit to the
assault and damage you can perpetrate on something so
very complex.

Stop thinking about insects as pests; put them in perspec-
tive, and it will probably help your attitude to them. They
are, after all, part of the system. Perhaps you are the
problem and not some poor bug. Maybe you've introduced
some imbalance to the garden that draws them inexorably.
It's pretty hard to *manage or control* creatures we don't
know all that much about.

If you choose strong healthy plants, put them in the right place, feed and water the soil properly, the amount of damage any pest can do is minimal. By interplanting flowers and vegetables, by companion planting, by growing a wide diversity of plants you will help your garden stay healthy. This is the preventative approach to gardening.

You will be hearing more and more about sustainable agriculture or permaculture (*perm*anent agri*culture*). Permaculture means redesigning our approach to the land. Not seeing it merely in terms of the tons of crops we produce, and the dollars we receive but of a more integrated approach. We may have to relearn all about the natural systems and how they function. We must learn how to imitate nature. It's not a them-and-us situation with bugs and diseases. If we change the way we approach pests in the garden this will, in the long run, encourage change in the way society sees agriculture. Short-term gain is not part of this system.

So don't look for the quick fix. Take the time to find out what role bugs have in the natural system. If you give the soil what it needs and you practise balanced fertilization (as in lots of composting) you'll eliminate many of your problems. Bugs can be informative. They're there for a reason. So instead of going on a rampage with spray can in hand, take what Eliot Coleman calls the cause-correction approach—be participatory rather than antagonistic. He calls it biological diplomacy. I call it preventative gardening— making the connections between your healthy soil, the right plants and the life cycles of insects—plant between cycles if you can.

I've tried just about every alternative form of pest control that I could find. Most have middling success. But the best, most effective way to deal with any kind of pest, I'm here to report, is the most conservative way possible:

handpicking. No quick fixes in that. Know your enemy. Be able to identify them, be aware of their habits. For instance, I've had a real hate on for earwigs but earwigs also eat aphid eggs and other spoilers so I stopped trying to get rid of all of them. They too have a proper place in the garden. I swear since I came to this conclusion there are fewer around or I just don't notice them any more. I certainly haven't been bitten by one recently.

I still follow well-entrenched habits: armed with flashlight I pick slugs up after twilight falls or in the first light of dawn. Call me sick but it gives me great pleasure picking the slimy little devils off plants and squishing them underfoot. Slug Patrol. I don't mind the goo on my hands and I've learned a lot about slugs in the process. One is that they move faster than you might suspect; two, they can dive down deep into the earth; and three, it must be incredibly cruel to throw them in a dish of salt to dry them right out. They writhe and, anthropomorphically I imagine, scream in sluggy agony. Not that I'm sentimental about slugs but it's faster grinding them under your heel anyway.

Conventional wisdom is that insect pests are symptoms of something else wrong in the garden. Perhaps there's something lacking in the soil, or in the way you planted or organized your garden. Look in that direction first. Remember the organic watchword: treat the soil not the plant. I have a healthy garden and I also have a lot of slugs. It depends on the weather. I also get leafminer on *Aquilegia*, mildew on the phlox. So I stomp on the slugs, cut the leaves off anything that looks like it has leafminer and move the phlox to places with better circulation.

Learn as much as you can about your plants; build up a healthy soil and follow these rules:
1. Pick off pests.
2. Create barriers with ashes or Diatomaceous Earth so they can't get at the plant.

3. Companion plant to repel the pests.

4. Mix a solution of soap and water in a spray bottle and make a direct blast on the offender.

5. Attract birds and beneficial bugs by planting what *they* like.

6. If you are desperate, use one of the botanicals listed, below.

ECOLOGICAL PESTICIDES

You are certainly going to hear more and more about these in the future. As the chemical companies do their best to green up, you'll be seeing "organic" on a lot of products. Be wary. No insecticide can really be called organic but some are acceptable in an organic system. For instance, fish emulsion and botanical powders do have some synthetic ingredients such as stabilizers. Botanical pesticides, derived from plants instead of chemicals, aren't necessarily safer but the effects are short-lived and they break down rapidly. They tend to disrupt the natural systems less violently, but some have a few problems of their own.

BACILLUS THURINGIENSIS (Bt) • is a natural bacterium that kills such caterpillar pests as cabbageworm, gypsy moth larvae and corn borer. It's generally considered about the best material you can use and is relatively benign.

DIATOMACEOUS EARTH • is the shells of one-celled plants called diatoms which lived millions of years ago. The fossilized remains became a fine chalk-like rock. It's sometimes used to filter wine. But Diatomaceous Earth has high levels of free silica. This can damage lungs, causing silicosis, so you must protect yourself when using it. Basalt dust does the same job and is safer. Both have microscopic needles that pierce soft-bodied insects and dehydrate them.

ROTENONE, RYANIA, SABADILLA AND PYRETHRUM • are organic products you should be careful of. They break down quickly enough but can be toxic to some beneficials, fish and humans if handled improperly.

POLITICALLY CORRECT SUPPLIES

- Insecticidal soap such as Safer's is your first line of defence in the war against pests. You have to have a keen eye, bathe leaves in the soap or make a direct hit on the bug. It won't hurt lady bugs and other beneficials.

Here are some other products recommended by *Organic Gardening* magazine:

- Safer's Clandosan 618 consists of chitin taken from shellfish wastes mixed with soybean meal and urea. When the chitin decomposes, it encourages beneficial fungi and the release of nitrogen which in turn is toxic to nematodes. Use it about three weeks before you plant. Bumping up the organic content of your soil will also help if you have sandy soil.
- Timed Release Indoor-Outdoor Insect Killer from Safer.
- Safer's Margosan-O slows the feeding of more than 150 insect pests. Won't hurt birds, mammals, butterflies or honeybees. Mealy bugs, army worms, loopers, sweet potato whitefly and gypsy moths will succumb.
- Snailer from Gardener's Supply uses yeast to attract and capture slugs.
- Slug-off is a herbal-oil and natural resins pellet that deters slugs.

- M-One contains Bt natural bacteria that causes leaf-eating caterpillars to die—this is a new strain.
- Biosafe Lawn & Garden Insect Control has nematodes that parasitize soil-dwelling insects such as black vine weevils (terrible for rhododendrons), web-worms, Japanese beetle grubs, billbugs, cutworms, mole crickets, cucumber beetle larvae and more. They contain symbiotic bacteria which propagate rapidly inside host insects and kill them. Reapply every 3 to 4 weeks. Nematodes can live 3-4 weeks without a host and can propagate without a food source.
- Dipel and Thuricide contain Bt in either liquid or powder form. Can be applied directly on the plant or soil. Breaks down in sunlight; reapply after rain.
- Fossil Flower and Puroguard contain Diatomaceous Earth.
- There are better horticultural oils now available—much lighter and less lethal. Check horticultural-oil labels—many of them are out-of-date. Newer oils can be applied even when temperatures drop below 40°F (5°C) but are not recommended above 90°F (32°C).
- Sunspray Ultra-Fine oil (Mycogen Corporation by Sun Refining Company): 2 percent solution applied during the growing season to woody ornamentals will protect against a wide range of pests (scale, spider mites, aphids and rust).
- Tanglefoot can be applied around trees to ward off caterpillars, ants and other ambulatory insects.

NONCOMMERCIAL ALTERNATIVES

I like these homemade products better than anything in a spray can. Even if the product is environmentally friendly, its container is still unrecyclable garbage. No matter which kind you use, commercial or homemade, don't go into a spray program during the blossom season or on any day that is not cool and still.

- Asparagus juice sprayed on tomato leaves will protect them from nematodes.
- Elderberry leaves: make an infusion by soaking overnight; sprinkle over roses and other flowers against blight.
- Garlic and horseradish extracts, and tannic acid are good repellents and may prevent insects from eating plants. But these are only temporary solutions.
- Garlic spray: soak 3-4 chopped garlic cloves in 2 tbsp. (30 grams) mineral oil for a day; add a pint (½ litre) of water; stir, strain; a dilute 1:20 water solution will zap most pests.
- Grind up two to four hot peppers with one small onion, a bulb of garlic, and 1 quart (1 litre) water; leave a day, then strain. Add enough water to make a gallon (4 litres). Bury the mash. A direct hit will dispatch ants, cabbageworms, spiders and caterpillars.
- Garlic and onion spray: grind together to make an effective general spray.
- Dried ground up hot pepper and dusted on tomato plants; cayenne pepper dusted on plants wet with dew is excellent against a caterpillar infestation.
- Crush the flowers of Pyrethrum, *Chrysanthemum coccineum*, in a blender with water; strain and use as a spray for aphids. This material is in many commercial blends and is perfectly safe. It's a beneficial botanical.
- Rhubarb: Boil leaves and sprinkle the tea on soil before sowing and it will prevent clubroot. Also useful against greenfly and black spot on roses.
- Soap: Mix 2 teaspoons (10 mL) Ivory with a gallon (4 litres) of warm water.

- Sugar kills nematodes. Apply 5 pounds (2.2 kilograms) to 100 pounds (45 kilograms) of soil. This will kill these pests in 24 hours.
- Sumac leaves contain tannin. Chop up leaves and bury sacks of them around apple trees infested with woolly aphids.
- Tansy: Mix one ounce of tansy (75 grams) with 1¼ cup (310 millilitres) (1:10) water. Process in a blender or food processor. Strain.
- Tomato leaves contain an active alkaloid. Chop up tomato leaves and soak in water. Spray the mixture against aphids on roses. Or boil stems and leaves in water; cool, strain. Spray on roses to destroy black or green flies and caterpillars.
- Wormwood, *Artemisia absinthum*: make a tea to spray on the ground in fall and spring to discourage slugs; spray on fruit trees to repel aphids.

A GARDEN FOR BENEFICIALS

A garden to attract the good bugs, or beneficials, will include: mulch for ladybird beetles, sugar for lacewings, ground cover for spiders and ground beetles and a patch of aromatic herbs for bees and hover flies. Remember that hybrid flowers won't attract bees, wasps or hover flies. They like bright-colored flowers of different sizes, blossom shapes and fragrance—geraniums, painted daisies, zinnias and weeds. Be sure to have a place for these bugs to drink. Let water sit long enough—at least an hour—to let chemicals such as chlorine evaporate before setting it out for these friends. Other methods of attracting beneficials:

- Make a barrier of sunflowers, small shrubs (roses, elder, blackberries) and trees around your garden. This will attract the ladybug and provide the right kind of habitat.

- Plant a strip of the following flowers: bee balm, comfrey, rudbeckia, butterfly bush. This mix will attract tachinid and syrphid flies.
- *COGnition* recommends: Planting a row of sunflowers and kochias. The latter is a 5-foot (150-centimetre) annual with red, green or yellow leaves that will help your self-cleaning garden, by reseeding and providing an insect barrier. They also recommend stacking the fibrous stalks of vegetables against this in the fall to attract ladybugs, which, in turn, are attracted to the bugs emerging from their stems. Everything can be composted in spring.
- Have a strip of grass running through your garden. Fill it with the right kind of weeds: Queen-Anne's lace, dandelions, clover. Bits of raised wood placed judiciously about will encourage spiders, ground beetles and praying mantises to come in to rest or to deposit eggs. The latter eat anything.
- Trap plants such as nasturtiums will attract aphids.
- Ants are repelled by pennyroyal, spearmint, southernwood and tansy. You also want to attract bats and birds.

Bats: Bats are prodigious eaters of insects. They can consume up to 5,000 insects every night. This includes grasshoppers, corn borers, cutworm moths. Don't worry about their droppings. They are no worse than most birds. We have lots of bats looping around our house and trees at night (a fact my kids kept secret for years) and I've never seen anything that even looks vaguely like bat guano. If you don't have the right habitat, put up a bat house to attract them to your garden. Since they are nocturnal, they aren't going to bother you much and they will keep your space free of mosquitoes.

Birds: • Birds eat grubs, beetles and flying insects.
- A combination of seeds and nuts; or a mix of sunflower seeds, millet, oats, corn; even sunflower seeds alone will attract just about every desirable bird.

- Almost any plant with red blossoms will attract birds.
- A bird bath will draw them as well as provide water for the good bugs.
- Get one of these dandy bird feeding stations that will close up shop when something heavier than a bird lands on it—something pesky like a squirrel.
- Trees and shrubs: a wild section will keep useful woodpeckers, chickadees, nuthatches in residence. If you leave animal hair, string and rags strategically placed, they will have something for nests.

Frogs and toads: If you can safely attract them to your garden they will eat up to 10,000 insects in three months. They consume grubs, cutworms, sow bugs, moths, flies, chinch bugs.

- Frogs will be more likely to hang about a pond.
- Toads are ground lovers and will need protection from the sun.

Herbs for Beneficials: anise, caraway, catnip, coriander, cumin, dill, fennel, lavender, sweet marjoram, mint, rosemary, autumn and pineapple sage, winter savory, tansy and thyme.

Flowers for beneficials: roses, *montbretia* (also known as *crocosmia*), wild flowers.

GOOD BUGS (ALSO KNOWN AS BENEFICIALS)

Bees as almost everyone knows are essential to life. They pollinate plants allowing them to bear fruit. No pollination, no plant life. They can see blue and yellow flowers but not red. They love the yellow-centred blossoms of fruit trees. Never spray the latter with dormant oil when the trees are blooming or you'll wipe out the bees. Other plants to consider: forsythia, pussy willow, Russian olive.

Monarda also known as bee balm for good reason; salvia; aster; annuals such as cleome are all attractive to bees as well. (See also *Companion Planting*, page 113.)

Assassin Bugs: eat caterpillars, Japanese beetles and leafhoppers.

Braconid Wasps: These tiny wasps will parasitize larvae of gypsy moths, codling moth, tent caterpillars, cutworms, strawberry leafroller and oriental fruit moth, all of which attract them. In areas where DDT hasn't been used, they can clean up the destructive gypsy moth.

Chalcid Wasps: They will devour mealybugs, aphids, scale, the larvae of moths, beetles and butterflies. You can buy these commercially and release them into your garden.

Damselflies destroy aphids, leafhoppers, tree-hoppers, small caterpillars.

Encarsia Wasps are parasitic to whiteflies.

Ichneumon Flies: When introduced they can clean up the spruce sawfly, wood-boring caterpillars, tomato moth.

Fireflies or lightning bugs feed on slugs and snails. They live in low vegetation.

Ground Beetles:

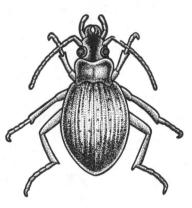

Ground beetle: A good bug, black with a slight iridescence; lives in the soil and eats a variety of plant pests.

Raised beds will attract these fierce looking beetles. I was terrified of them until I found out they were A Good Thing. They are big and black with a slight iridescence—a shiny dark green tinge on the thorax—and purple elsewhere. Leave them alone. They are not to be confused with June beetles which are less rounded and much bigger. During the day, they live in soil, and if you stir them up they scurry for cover. They eat loads of slugs, and go after gypsy moth larvae, cankerworms, armyworms and cutworms.

Hover Flies: Plants to attract them—baby blue eyes, cosmos, marigold, meadow foam, *Limnanthes Douglasii*, spearmint, all members of the daisy family.

Lacewings:

Lacewing: A beneficial bug, active at night, that eats many small insect pests.

Attracted to all members of the carrot family: Queen-Anne's lace, wild lettuce or oleander, red cosmos, angelica, goldenrod and tansy. A light will draw the nocturnally active creature which eats aphids, spidermites, leafhoppers, thrips, moth eggs, red mites and caterpillars.

Ladybird Beetles (ladybugs): If lady beetles or ladybugs need any identification, just look on the cover of this book. They are probably everyone's favorite bug. The larvae of this most useful of all bugs can down 25 aphids a day, the adult 56 a day. And one coupling will produce from 200 to 1,000 offspring. They can get into areas no spray could possibly penetrate. Plant angelica, butterfly weed, nasturtium, marigold, tansy, evergreen euonymus, goldenrod, morning-glory and yarrow to attract them into your garden.

• If you buy ladybugs, try to get those raised locally. The ones from the mountains won't stay in your garden. Unless you've got the right habitat, ladybugs go into decline, or they'll leave your garden for one that suits them better.

Parasitic Wasps: *trichogramma* is a parasite that destroys the eggs of many moths, butterflies and loopers. They appreciate a wildflower assortment—any nectar-producing flowers with an open single flower; members of the carrot and daisy family, buttercup, goldenrod, strawberries and white clover.

Phytis Wasps: attack scale insects.

Praying Mantis:

Praying Mantis: A useful bug, often found in clumps of brambles. Attacks its prey and devours it for food.

Likes clumps of goldenrod, cosmos, raspberries and other brambles. It looks a bit like a grasshopper with strong front legs (hence the praying position they seem to take). They are dormant from the beginning of November to middle of May. They can clean up your garden but might also eat some of the beneficials. Eggs are laid in fall, hatch in May and June, mature through the summer, and die in fall. First food is aphids, then leafhoppers, and in adulthood chinch bugs, crickets, caterpillars, leafhoppers.

Rove Beetle: has a long dark, flat body a bit like an earwig without the curved appendages at the stern. Destroys red spider, cabbage maggots and larvae of cabbage fly.

Syrphid flies: (or flower flies) are aphid predators that look like wasps, and feed on pollen and nectar. If your rose bush is infested with aphids, they'll find them and wipe them out in a few days (eating an aphid a minute). Any member of the huge daisy family will attract them. In addition, they love leafhoppers, mealybugs, spiders, mites and scale.

Tachinid Flies: wild buckwheat attracts them. They look like house flies but they muck about around flowers drinking up nectar. Some inject caterpillar hosts with maggots. They can destroy larvae of browntail and gypsy moths, sawflies, cutworms, armyworms and Mexican bean beetles.

BAD BUGS

These insects are the ones that irritate us the most because they chew up our plants, mess up the lawn and generally misbehave—at least by human standards. One of the simplest ways of dealing with them, apart from handpicking or direct sprays of water, is to plant trap crops. These are plants that will attract the nuisances away from other plants to themselves. *Voilà!* you've got them all in one place. So when you hear that nasturtiums are a pain in the neck because they get covered with aphids, it's not quite true. They are drawing them away from all the other plants in the garden making it easier for you to catch them *en masse*. You can be sure, however, that if you do get an infestation, predators will move in pretty quickly.

Good drainage is essential for controlling pests. Don't leave wet stuff around for long. Clean up dead leaves and foliage from around plants. Keep your plants hosed down if you do notice some tiny blighter on the attack.

A general rule for flying insects is to make your own controls. They are attracted to yellow. Construct sticky papers; recycle yellow plastic jugs by cutting out circles and covering with Tanglefoot paste (this is a balsam resin); hang them around the garden.

Ants: Not all ants are bad; they destroy larvae of house and fruit flies. They help the opening of peony buds. I love watching the stroking motions of the ants as they sip on the sap of the buds. It won't hurt the plant so leave them alone. Ants also help aerate the soil and of course eventually become humus. But if you are overrun, try the following:
• Sage, lavender and hyssop will keep them away.
• If they are infesting your roses, make a tea of ferns and pour it around the affected plants.
• Strawberries attract ants—make a tea of southernwood and pour over the plants when it is cool.
• Plant spearmint or tansy near the kitchen to keep them away.

Black ants: In the house—in an old lid put 1 tsp (5 mL) rotenone, add 1 tsp (5 mL) honey, 1 tsp (5 mL) water. Place in the cupboard or any area ants seem to be congregating.

Carpenter ants: They have a bad reputation as chewers of wood but what they really indicate is that you have a problem—not that they are the problem. They nest where wood has already disintegrated. Plant aromatic tansy by all doors; Diatomaceous Earth sprinkled along their path will dry them out.

Fire ants: Pour 1 tbsp (15 mL) Borax on the ant hill to keep them in check. Make a manure tea and pour it over the hill; mix 2 tsp (10 mL) Borax in a pint ($^1/_2$ litre) of apple jelly and drop the sticky stuff around the mound—workers will carry it to the queen and it will kill her.

Aphids:

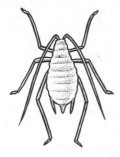

Aphid: Greatly enlarged. Nearly every species of plant is adversely affected by some species of aphid.

Beneficials: ladybird beetle, green lacewing, syrphid fly, hover fly, flower fly or parasitic wasp.

Trap plants: nasturtiums, plantain and lamb's-quarters will attract them away from other plants for easy handpicking.

* Chives, garlic, pennyroyal (a creeping mint), southernwood, nasturtium, coriander, tansy and anise act as repellents.

   Most types of aphids can overwinter. They are 1/10 (.25 centimetre) to 1/5 (.51 centimetre) of an inch (2.5 centimetres) long and can produce up to 20 populations a year. They are visible on leaves and shoots and the sticky honeydew sometimes becomes covered in sooty moulds. Look for gall-like swellings on leaves; curling, sometimes yellow, leaves. By sucking the sap, aphids cause withering of foliage. The honeydew is exuded from the anus. This gets all over the surface, turns it sticky and blocks out the sun. This in turn produces black mould which blocks out even more sun. The disease is carried from plant to plant by the winged form of aphids. Ants herd aphids to keep them together for the honeydew. You can spot them this way.

* Preventative measures: Clean up. Don't leave discarded plants around. Thoroughly cultivate areas where you've had to remove plants.

* Aphids may indicate low nitrogen content in your soil.

- Dust plants with baking powder on the undersides.
- If they infect apple, quince or pear, use one of the new dormant-oil sprays in spring (not during the blossom season of course).
- Chalcid wasp is the only insect predator for the woolly apple aphid.
- Aphids on rose bushes: Sprinkle soap and water mixture on them. Use your hands to rub them off, then hose the plant down.
- Plant garlic beside your rose bushes to keep down aphids. Do this with your houseplants as well.
- Be sure to check under the leaves if you have these little devils—that's where they lay their eggs. And they over-winter very successfully.
- Clean off the infected plant with a hose or spray with insecticidal soap. Then brush Diatomaceous Earth on the leaves.
- Make your own aphid traps—paint yellow cardboard with Tanglefoot, and hang it near the plant. Use a yellow dish (obviously the animal likes yellow) and fill it with soapy water.
- Mince shallots in a food processor and make a spray; do the same with rhubarb leaves—boil half an hour in 3 quarts (3 litres) water, add one quart (1 litre) water when cool. Dissolve one ounce (2.54 grams) soap flakes in the mix—this will help it adhere to the plant. You can make a substitute with elder leaves (this will also discourage mildew on roses).
- Spray with a strong solution of limewater.
- Take tomato leaves and chop, add 1 quart (1 litre) of boiling water, and steep. Strain. Dilute with water 4:1 and spray.
- To discourage winged aphids, put sheets of aluminum foil around plants—the reflection of the sky will confuse them.

- Grind up hot pepper and mix with black pepper. Cut with water and spray every three days directly on the aphids.
- Use rotenone as a last resort.

Chinch Bugs: A pain in eastern North America. They hibernate in grass and the damage to lawns is caused by the young which are 1/5 to 1/4 inch (5 to 6 millimetres) long, reddish in color. The adults are black with a white spot between the wings on the back. Yellowing grass, then dead patches, will tip you off. Or you'll smell them when you walk across the lawn.

Make a test: cut out the end of a large can and push it into the soil. Fill with water and any chinch bugs in the soil will float to the surface. They have a natural predator in the bigeyed bug. You will have to cut out the infected areas and then reseed.

Colorado Potato Beetle:

Colorado Potato Beetle: Found on the undersides of potato leaves, eggplant, peppers and tomatoes.

Beneficial: ground beetle.

These insects are 1/3 inch (.8 cm) long with a hard convex brownish red shell and yellow stripes. The eggs are yellow-orange and will be found on the undersides of potato leaves, eggplant, peppers and tomatoes. Hand pick all three—larvae, eggs and beetles—or knock them into a container of water with a little detergent added.

- Interplant affected areas with garlic or marigolds.
- Hand pick the yellow eggs, or the larvae.
- Squish the cluster of jelly-like orange eggs between fingers. Or fill a pail half-full of water with 1 tbsp

(15 mL) cooking oil. Put under the plant and gently shake the beetles into the bucket.
- Make your own bug juice of larvae and beetles mixed with water.
- Fossil Flower will penetrate larvae.
- Dust with rotenone or Diatomaceous Earth (usual rules apply—wear protective clothing).
- Bacillus thuringiensis (Bt) will attack the larvae.

Cutworms:

Beneficials: trichogramma wasps, fireflies, tachinid flies and ground beetles.
- Tansy will repel them.

These are the caterpillars of the night-flying moth. They are grey-brown, one inch (2.5 centimetres) long and will curl up if disturbed or feeding (loves to curl around the stem of new tomato plants). Overwinters as young larvae.

You can tell they are lurking about when you see the tops of young plants lopped off.
- Protect new plants by putting toothpicks on either side of the stem.
- Use collars of paper or cardboard around young transplants.
- Use oak leaf mulch along garden paths.
- Pick them off plants at night.
- Put bran meal around transplants or try a mix of sawdust and bran with enough molasses to make a sticky goo. When they climb off the plant, they are trapped in the muck.
- Circle plants with wood ashes from the fireplace.
- Spray Bacillus thuringiensis (Bt) around transplants.

Earwigs:

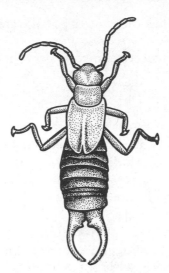

Earwig: Both adults and young are nocturnal, and feed on worms, small insects and young plants.

Beneficials: tachinid fly and syrphid flies will devour earwig eggs. These reddish-brown insects with their pincer-shaped claws on the abdomen are mean. They bite. They lay their white eggs in the soil and overwinter in this state. You'll notice their presence by holes in flowers and foliage. Earwigs are nocturnal creatures and they like to find a dark moist place to sleep in during the day. If you have a large infestation be careful with your mulching. Mulch provides the perfect resting spot but it's also a good place to catch them.

• Don't erase them from your garden; they eat aphids and other little sucking insects. But they also like fresh new leaves, especially cotyledons—the first two leaves of a new plant.

• Traps: an old pipe, garden hose or a rolled up umbrella left out for them to rest in during the day will attract

them. Then dunk them into a pail of water (coat the sides with a bit of salt or soap so they can't escape).
- Half bury a small container of beer. They will fall in and die boozing.
- Often they'll crawl into a bucket of soapy water and drown.
- If they happen to get into the house—they love to lie between sheets at the cottage in my experience—use Diatomaceous Earth (DE). If you have pets or children, put a small container of DE inside a cupboard or under the sink. Sprinkle around cracks.
- Dust with rotenone or DE.

Grasshoppers: *Nosema locustae*, a protozoan parasite which attacks grasshoppers and some species of crickets. Dissolve in water, add bran and put around the garden. They eat and die and pass it on to the next generation.

Japanese Beetle: This blue, iridescent beetle can be treated with rotenone (Fossil Flower).
- Milky spore disease is also very effective.
- Traps can be made with geranium oil.
- Plant African marigolds and evening primrose. The beetles will be poisoned by castor bean plant leaves, and blossoms of white geraniums.

Leafminers:
Beneficials: Robins, purple finches and chickadees love leafminers. Encourage then with a birdbath or some other source of water. Trap plants: Radishes and lamb's-quarters. Plant about 15 feet (5 metres) away from an infected border. Keep picking away at them by scratching off the eggs (they are hatched when leaves develop grey blisters).

You can tell when these little devils are infecting your plants when white or brown tunnels or blotches appear on the leaves. I get them on my columbines. It would be nice to stop them before they do this damage but it's the larvae that do the tunnelling and by the time you see little black flies with yellow stripes, it's too late. They emerge in spring and lay eggs throughout the summer and may carry diseases with them.

- Cut off any blistered leaves and get rid of them. Leave enough healthy tissue so that the plant isn't harmed.
- Handpicking is best: turn leaves of vulnerable plants over and look for chalky white eggs 1/6 to 1/8 inch (.4-.3 cm) long.

Mealybugs:
Beneficials: chalcid wasps, cryptolaemus beetle and lacewing larvae. There are short- and long-tail versions of these pests. They appear as clusters of white, waxy fluff on stems and on bottom leaves.

- Clean off leaves by a direct hit with the hose.
- Clean top and bottom with insecticidal soap or any soap and water concoction.
- Use a watercolor brush dipped in alcohol to remove from houseplants.

Mite, Red Spider Mite *see* Spider Mites
Nematodes
Most nematodes are useful but there are some wormy minuscule creatures that inject toxins into plants. The plant becomes stunted, leaves turn yellow.

Trap plant: Castor beans.

- Marigolds, *Tagetes patula* attract nematodes and then release a substance that kills them off. Let the plants decay in the soil. Mustards, smartweed, wild chicory, and chrysanthemums such as feverfew and painted daisy will also help.
- Best bet to clear up this problem is a good compost of leaf mould and kelp. Mix into the soil.
- Mulch with pine leaves.
- Fish emulsion repels nematodes. Use as a foliar spray.

Slugs and Snails: You're always reading about how to get rid of slugs and earwigs in magazines and organic publications—just put out a board and collect them in the morning. Well, my garden won't hold a lot of boards. What I find most effective, especially given the way I garden, is to leave a small pile of garden detritus, preferably a little on the moist side, overnight. In the early morning, I lift the pile and stomp over any little creatures I find.

It's the little ones that do the most damage so don't be fooled by size. They live in damp sheltered places the year round, rest during the day and come out to dine at night.

One of my favorite magazines is *The Island Grower* and they tell me that slugs can be eliminated in three years by assiduous handpicking. You have to do this every day and keep a pretty clean garden. You can use this in conjunction with other methods of course.

One old book recommends making a "dead line" of salt—they can't go past and survive. Salt, of course, is sure death for slugs because it dries out their slimy little bodies. *Beneficials*: Larvae of lightning bugs, garter snakes, rove and ground beetles, ducks, box turtles and salamanders.

- Slug Traps: Slice up potatoes, carrots, cabbage or lettuce leaves for them to feed on and they might leave other plants alone. Then get after them with your stomping slippers.
- One gardener I know pierces slugs with a sharpened stick with a 12-inch (30-centimetre) needle-sharp spike on the end—slug shishkabob. To keep slugs away from her beans: she digs a metal pole (an old pipe will do) about 6 or 7 feet (2 metres) long securely into the soil and puts a hub cap with a dozen holes drilled around the perimeter on it. She runs string from the hub cap holes down to tent-pegs on the ground. Then she puts slug bait all around and gets slug-free scarlet runners.

- Here's another strategy: don't mulch stuff that slugs are after, use Diatomaceous Earth (DE) or ashes or something sharp and pointed around the plants once you've cleaned up. If the slugs persist, hand pick faithfully every day.
- Be sure to mulch around plants *after* the first frost and after you've cleaned up around the plants.
- When things cool off in the fall, slugs will search for protection (boards, large leaves, garden debris) and this is the time to make a great haul.
- Use protective borders of sand, ashes, lime, or metal barriers—this assumes that they are outside the border trying to get in.
- Slugs don't like oak leaves or wood shavings.
- Hellebore keeps slugs from grape vines.
- The traditional beer mix draws them out of their lairs. Put a cut-down yogurt or margarine container in a shallow hole so that it's even with the ground. Pour in beer and a little water. Use the top to partially cover and to keep rain out. If they tend to leave after drinking, add a little flour to make the mixture sticky.
- Here's a variation from Canadian Organic Growers: To a 1 lb (500 g) plastic container half-full of water, add 1 tbsp (15 mL) brewer's yeast, 1 tbsp (15 mL) molasses or honey, 1 tbsp (15 mL) cooking oil. This mixture will keep both slugs and earwigs from escaping. If they're all dead, put them in the compost.
- Copper wire and crushed eggshells strewn around plants will deter slugs to some degree but remember that they can go underground.
- Make collars of window screen to keep them away from the stems of plants.
- Try sprinkling powdered ginger around plants.

- Or create a slug fence by using 3 inches (7.5 centimetres) of screen pushed into the ground about an inch (2.5 centimetres) with the top facing out. Slugs caught inside the fence will be easy enough to pick out and no others will get inside.
- Cover with a 2-inch (5-centimetre) layer of compost and top up with sawdust—they hate things with sharp ends. Then trace a border with wood ashes.
- Fertosan Slug Destroyer and Snailproof are two acceptable commercial preparations.

Sow Bugs:

These little guys look like something left over from the last ice age. They have an armor-like crust, seven pairs of legs and perpetually gobble up decaying matter. They look like pillbugs, but when discovered the pillbug curls up; the sowbug runs for cover.

- Pyrethrum will get rid of them if they're a problem. But oak leaf mulch, wood ashes in the soil, a lime solution—1 pound in 5 gallons of water (.5 kilograms in 22 litres) will help. They won't damage the compost pile, but discourage them by turning it frequently. Make sure there aren't any in the compost that you spread around the garden.
- Sprinkle with a little lime.
- Hand pick; use Diatomaceous Earth (DE) or ashes; don't mulch.

Spider Mite:

Beneficials: lacewings, ladybugs, predatory mites (which are also commercially available).

Leaves become mottled, turn bronze, and fall prematurely. The reddish-brown spidery adults are so tiny, about the size of a grain of salt, that you'll only know you've got them when you see a fine webbing of white in leaves and stems. They feed on leaves, fruit and roots.

Leaves curl up and turn yellow. Eggs are laid on the leaves or buds close to the base of the plant.

- They like an arid atmosphere. Keep plants shady, and cool by misting.
- Use insecticidal soap cut with seaweed solution and spray on undersides of new growth regularly every two weeks.
- Spray directly with a jet of water.
- Mix whole wheat flour, buttermilk and water and wash off with this goo.
- Dust sulphur on both sides of the leaves before temperatures reach 90°F (32°C).
- They are repelled by onion, garlic, chives.
- Botanicals: use pyrethrum in a spray directly on mites on the underside of leaves four days apart; or, sabadilla dusted on plants after a heavy dew or shower.
- Diatomaceous Earth dusted on plants also helps.
- Use one of the new superior dormant oil sprays on fruit trees in fall. It will suffocate the spider mites and keep them from wintering over.
- A 2 percent oil of coriander mixed with water solution, or 2 percent emulsion of oil of lemon grass make effective sprays.

Tent Caterpillar: Found in fruit trees both domestic and wild. Eastern Tent Caterpillar: yellowish brown to dark brown with two white stripes on each wing. They appear in seven to ten year cycles. They straddle trees with cases of eggs laid in the fall and overwinter. It's the larvae, black caterpillars with whitish stripes down the back, that do the damage.

Beneficial: parasitic wasps depending on your area. Baltimore Orioles will clean them up.

- Strike when you see the first tents form; pull them out by hand. Or destroy the egg masses in winter.

- In spring get rid of the new webs by wiping with a kerosene-soaked cloth — don't light it.
- Spray caterpillars with Bacillus thuringiensis (Bt).
- Dust with Diatomaceous Earth. Forest Tent Caterpillar: has a row of orange spots along its back. Found, obviously, in the forest.

Animal Pests: Any of these animals may invade your garden. I'm on an ancient racoon path and I know that they will always be there. I've watched people put out traps and carry them off, but I worry about separating mothers and babies. My cat, for crying out loud, entertains them at night. Sometimes there'll be five out on the back deck. I swear it's in their genes that they have a right to stroll through my garden. I give up. You can try and animal-proof your garden: keep all fences in good repair; patch cracks and holes in wood. Good luck.

Birds:
- To discourage pigeons, starlings, and other irritating birds, place weatherproof netting over any edges they fancy perching along.

Cats: I'm a cat person and even though I adore her, Mickie (my own ball of fluff) can be a pain in the neck when she decides to sleep on top of a particularly favored heath. Why this plant? I don't know. A series of small sharp sticks will keep her out of most parts of the garden.

Dogs: If you don't own one, they can be a drag. I have a regular who urinates on plants near the sidewalk (watched over by doting owner). I've taken to sprinkling cayenne pepper over the spot which does discourage it from using the same spot over and over. I'm told that Epsom Salts sprinkled at the front of a border will help. Pound small sticks a foot or so apart around an area to keep them from trampling through easily.

Deer:

- Spray plants with a solution of six fresh eggs to 1 gallon (4 litres) of water and put it around the base of trees, and on grasses and shrubs along trails. Renew spray after rain.
- Protect roses by breaking a whole egg beneath the bushes—it gets smelly but not too offensive to humans.
- Make a fence 6 to 8 feet (2 to 2.5 metres) high with a 3 foot (1 metre) wide arbor on top. Stretch chicken wire on the ground beyond the outside of the fence.
- One of the garden gurus, Francisca Darts, has a huge garden in Surrey, British Columbia; she hangs Lifebuoy in old panty hose around the perimeter to keep them out. She isn't sure why Lifebuoy works better than other soaps, but it does.
- Bags of human hair outlining your territory will also help.
Gophers:
- If they are pernicious, grow your plants in 5-gallon (20-litre) plastic buckets. Remove the bottoms and drill holes in the sides; then bury them in spring. For small plants use berry baskets.
- Most of the suggestions for getting rid of gophers are so cruel I cannot even begin to record them. It's better to find natural predators such as dogs, hawks, snakes or skunks.

Groundhogs: A really good fence or treatment equally cruel as getting rid of gophers. If you go the fence route, you'll have to sink it fairly far into the ground.
- Plant a separate area of the garden for these animals. They like clover and alfalfa.
- Keep a section around the garden mowed.
- Natural predators are cats, dogs and hawks.

Mice: I've never really had a problem with mice but Caper Spurge, *Euphorbia Lathyrus*, will help deter them. Be careful of all the euphorbias; they can cause dermatitis if you handle them incorrectly.

- Borders of daffodils, narcissi, scilla and grape hyacinth will also discourage mice.
- Make sure that you keep areas around fruit trees free of mulch. In fact don't mulch any place mice like to nest until after the ground is frozen solid.
- Use plastic tree guard strips or aluminum foil to protect trees.
- Cats, snakes and owls are natural enemies of mice.

Moles: May mean you are infested with all sorts of snails, ants, bees, wasps, centipedes and grubs which they enjoy eating. In some ways they are really doing you a favor but they can destroy root systems and spread plant diseases. At freeze-up, all this life retreats deeper down in the soil, and the moles follow, aerating and moving humus into the subsoil.

- Whenever one gardener I know sees a mound of dirt rising up, she pokes a stick down the hole, enlarges it, then drops a couple of moth balls down there. Mothballs aren't environmentally friendly so I don't have them around. But then I don't have moles either.
- Elder repels moles.
- Caper Spurge, *Euphorbia Lathyrus*, also known as mole plant will fend off moles and is poisonous to them.
- Dump Kitty Litter into their holes (dirty not clean).
- Get a cat.

Rabbits:
- Scatter onions, blood meal, cayenne and wood ashes around plants.
- If you are bothered terribly, build an 18-inch (45-centimetre) fence and remember they will dig under if you've got something in there they love.

Raccoons: Nothing, I'm convinced, will discourage them. *You* might try, however, putting up flimsy fences around vegetable patches. Something high enough and tottery enough so they'll fall off when they reach the top.

- They like searching for grubs, which means that when they see freshly dug earth they go there immediately. They are lazy devils.
- Sprinkle blood meal around; renew after a rain or watering.
- Try hot cayenne pepper.
- I use stones or flat rocks to protect newly planted lilies from curious claws.
- Strew hydrated lime around whatever you value most. Be sure to reapply after a rainstorm.
- If you have a pond or fountain, they'll mess about in it. Drape netting material over it at night secured by rocks if they are a real nuisance. Otherwise be prepared for general cleanups.
- A small electric fence switched on at night is effective if not particularly attractive.
- Flashing lights will keep them away from the garden.
  Skunks:
- Build a wire mesh fence 3 feet (1 metre) high and 6 inches (15 cm) underground.
- Sprinkle cayenne pepper around the perimeter of the garden.
  Squirrels: We must be going through a population explosion. They are so aggressive they'll come right in the house if I leave the screen open. A friend refers to them as tree rats.
- Remove any place they can make nests, such as wood piles or heaps of debris.
- Get a dog.
- If you trap, get a humane trap and check on it regularly. But don't trap in spring when you could separate mother and babes. Release within its range. Unfortunately as you remove them, more squirrels will move in to take their place. Either give them handouts in one part of the garden or plant enough stuff to share.

- Be sure to scatter blood meal all over the place after planting bulbs. It will discourage squirrels and act as a fertilizer, but must be replenished each time it rains. And it will make a dog sick if it happens to be using your yard as a loo.
- Cayenne pepper is effective as well.
- Plant a moth ball alongside each bulb. Don't bother placing them on top of the ground; that just seems to indicate where something delicious is buried.
- Some recommend planting bulbs then covering the area with chicken wire. I'd worry about getting scratched but if you're careful this could be effective.
- When planting tulips or lilies, both of which squirrels adore, accompany them with either Crown Imperial, *Fritillaria imperialis*, or narcissi. The first smells skunky and the latter is poisonous to them.

• • •

If you are really bothered by the bugs in your garden or you can't identify them, send a sample to one of the following and be sure to ask for organic results.

Newfoundland and Labrador
Research Station
Agriculture Canada
P.O. Box 7098
St. John's, Nfld. A1E 3Y3

Prince Edward Island
Prince Edward Island Department of Agriculture
Master Gardener Program
P.O. Box 1600, Research Station
Charlottetown, P.E.I. C1A 7N3

Nova Scotia
Horticulture and Biology Branch
Nova Scotia Department of Agriculture and Marketing

P.O. Box 550
Truro, N. S. B2N 5E3

New Brunswick
Plant Industry Branch
Department of Agriculture
P.O. Box 6000
Fredericton, N.B. E3B 5H1

Quebec
National Identification Service
Room 3119
K.W. Neatby Building
Ottawa, Ont. K1A 0C6

Ontario
Pest Diagnostic Advisory Clinic
Room B14 Graham Hall
University of Guelph
Guelph, Ont. N1G 2W1

Manitoba
Manitoba Agriculture Entomology
Section 911-401 York Avenue
Winnipeg, Man. R3C 0P8

Saskatchewan
Meewasin Garden Line
Department of Horticulture
University of Saskatchewan
Saskatoon, Sask. S7N 0W0

Alberta
Alberta Environmental Centre
Plant Services Division
Bag 4000
Vegreville, Alta. T0B 4L0

British Columbia
Syd Cannings
Department of Zoology
University of British Columbia
Vancouver, B.C. V6T 2A9

CHAPTER FIVE

DISEASES AND DEFICIENCIES

WHEN YOU LOOK THROUGH GARDENING BOOKS from the 40s and 50s, you wonder how we have survived environmentally at all. No wonder gardeners have a terrible reputation as serious polluters who pour toxic chemicals all over their plants. We're still stuck with many of these chemicals. DDT, for instance, has been banned for many years, but traces of it remain in treated soil and water. And the thousands of other registered chemicals will also be with us — in the soil, the water table, or in our lakes and streams. By being an ecological gardener, you are at least fighting chemical technology. But don't be surprised if somehow somewhere no matter how hard you try, these pernicious toxics find a way into your garden.

Do you know if the nursery or plant breeder where you buy plants uses chemicals? If so, which ones? For this reason, I've tried in recent years to grow some of the more interesting plants from seed, or trade with other organic gardeners. But if you can't always do this, try to encourage your nursery to use as many alternatives to toxic chemicals as possible.

Rule of thumb in the garden: If you learn about some new bug or disease even if you've never seen it before, you'll suddenly find it lurking about your garden. It's true. No disease touched my garden until I started studying them. Then all of a sudden there they were right under my nose. My general theory had been if a plant was fussy it probably didn't want to live with me. But as I've raised more and more plants, I've become quite possessive about them. I don't want slugs and earwigs munching away on them, and I certainly don't want them contracting unnecessary diseases. Much like children they are. The very best way to keep disease out of the garden is to follow a few sensible rules:

- Soil: Healthy soil is imperative in keeping disease away.
- Compost: This is the next most important factor—compost—rotted compost at that. The components in compost are anathema to fungal disease and some bacterial diseases. Low temperature compost, though it takes much longer to produce, has even more disease-resistant elements than does high temperature compost. You might want to have both kinds if you have the room.
- Mulching: This will help suppress weeds, keep the soil warm at night, cool during the day, and hold in moisture. And avoid damage through freeze-thaw cycles during the winter.

PREVENTATIVE GARDENING

Naturally, prevention is best; if you have healthy soil it will fight off disease. That means giving it enough water, enough drainage and enough fertilizer. An inch of compost a year is asking a lot but that will keep your soil extremely happy.

There are many reasons why your plants might contract an illness. It could be the weather or pollution. The disease might be from a virus, a bacteria or fungi. It's not easy to tell. Diseases come in three forms:

Bacterial diseases: often caused by persistent humidity, wet soil and high temperatures. Bacteria are invisible plants that live in both animals and plants. Bacteria that live on dead plants are called saprophytes. Those that cause diseases are parasites or pathogens. They move through the soil by water or when the soil is disturbed. They can enter plants through wounds or natural openings and swim with the sap. Be sure to wash your tools with bleach (cut with water 1:4). If you touch these plants, wash your hands so you don't spread the disease. Get rid of leaves. Mulching can reduce the spread of bacterial disease. Bacterial diseases can cause:

Rot: slimy leaves, branches, tubers.

Wilt: pathogens block the vascular system.

Gall: overgrowth of cells affected by pathogens.

Good bacteria: Bacillus thuringiensis is used to knock down many different kinds of loopers, moths, borers, caterpillars. Any form loses strength in sunlight. It isn't harmful to either plants or humans.

Fungal diseases: Fungi take their energy from organic matter. They feed on live matter parasitically and are real trouble makers. Those that live on dead matter are saprophytic and helpful in breaking down material. And naturally occurring fungi keep many insect populations under control. Sanitation is your first line of defence against fungal diseases:

Downy mildew: powder patches on leaves.

Powdery mildew: fungi live on the surface and suck out nutrients from there.

Rust fungi: pustules of color.

Leaf spot fungi: yellow to green spots.

Fungal diseases spread slowly over weeks. In fact, by the time you notice some of them it's almost too late.

• To be effective as a preventative, use fungicides on plants which had it the year before. You might tag them or make a list to help you remember. Sulphur rock will prevent germination of some fungal spores. If temperatures are below 80°F (27°C), you can use it every two weeks. You have to be sure that you cover the plant. It only works where it hits.

- Water vulnerable plants deeply during the spring. If the roots get too dry and there is a heavy dew, fungi have the perfect opportunity to get started.
- Don't plant too close. Thin out surplus stems of plants such as Michaelmas daisies. Air must get to the back of stems.
- Get badly infected sections of plants right out of the garden.

Viral diseases: These are the most difficult to diagnose. No one is sure whether they are living organisms or non-living chemicals, according to *The Organic Gardening Encyclopedia*, because they can behave either way. Plants can get viruses from people, insects, tools or anything else that comes in contact with soil or plants.

Mosaic: green and yellow mottling of leaves from chlorosis (lack of chlorophyll).

Yellowing, leaf curl or too much branch might mean a plant's got a viral disease.

Nematodes: These are pathogens. They look like tiny worms and they can be lethal when they suck sap from the inside of a plant. Known also as roundworm or eelworm. There are about 500,000 species (who counts these things?). Most are good, but some are very bad. Symptoms include malformation of leaves, flowers, stems, dieback, yellow foliage.

If it appears that some disease is affecting your plant, maybe you are giving it too much or too little of something. Your soil is often the best way to cure a sick plant. After you've checked that a plant has the right light requirement, enough water and mulch, try the following:

Lack of nitrogen: loss of normal green color, pale.

- Plant might turn pale if you've added organic matter before the poor thing was mature enough. The bacteria will use up the nitrogen in the decomposition process, thus starving the plant.
- Spindly yellow leaves, then as the plant gets older the leaves turn reddish or purple and fall off prematurely. Use a little nitrogen, and note for next season if this happens late in the year.
- As a remedy for lack of nitrogen, give your plants a hit of any of the following: hoof and horn meal, blood meal or well-rotted manure (though this is lower than the other two in nitrogen content).

Lack of phosphorus: leaves turn reddish, blue-green or purple; are weak; attacked by insects or disease; or have brown spots.

- Add bone meal, organic matter, rock phosphates, fish emulsion or well-finished compost.

Lack of potassium: stunted growth in stems and roots with poor development of flowers, fruits and seeds. Leaf color may be bluish with browning leaf tips; yellow between veins; and brown spots. Leaves turn brown at the edges or curl up.

- When the lower leaves start turning yellow but the green veins are still apparent, there is a problem. Try dolomitic limestone, or just trowel on the compost.
- Add wood ashes, granite dust, finely ground potash rocks, sheep manure. Calcium or magnesium will help make potassium available.

Iron deficiency: Manifested by yellowed leaves in acid-loving plants.

- Add blood meal, manure or a high-nitrogen material, such as peat moss, oak leaves, pine needles, or finely powdered sulphur.

- Rusty nails around the roots of roses will help keep them healthy.
- Change the color of the blossoms of wisteria from white to purple by adding rusty nails, or iron filings.
  Trace minerals
- Compost will provide copper, zinc, manganese, and zinc. The leaves of trees with deep roots in your pile will also help.
- Lack of magnesium: leaves turn yellow, die and fall off. Leaves are necessary to form chlorophyll so be careful if leaves fall in significant numbers.
- Lack of calcium: distortion and rolling of younger leaves; poor root development.

Some other problems:

Yellowing of leaves: could also mean that there's a lack of light, of certain nutrients, or temperatures that are simply too high for the plant to withstand.

Yellowing between leaves: could also mean infestation by spider mites, or that pollution is affecting the plant.

Dead areas on leaves or tips: could mean that there's too much boron in the soil; too much fluoride in your water supply (in which case let the water sit for at least an hour before using); or spider mites.

Spots on leaves: too cold water, leafminer larvae.

Spots on edges and inner sections: cool temperatures, cold water, air pollution, too much light.

Now having said all that, too much of a good thing *can* also harm your plants. You can use too much manure or peat moss which will make the soil too rich for the plants it supports. Peat mulch doesn't help peonies, for instance. Dress with manure and bone meal; make sure the mixture doesn't come in contact with the crown. Irises are prone to crown rot so use rock phosphate and bone meal, but no manure.

- Blood meal makes a rich soil. Keep that in mind when you're sprinkling it around bulbs to keep squirrels away.

SPECIFIC DISEASES

Black Spot of Roses Symptoms: Reddish to black spots on the leaves which turn yellow and fall off. At the beginning a few spots appear, then little black pimply-type lesions; this means the spores are about to take off. Get them first. Weakens plants (which need the leaves to produce food for the blooms).

- Plant parsley near roses to keep off black spot.
- Don't plant too many roses prone to this disease together. Mix up varieties that are tolerant with those that are intolerant.
- Get all the leaves off the soil as quickly as they fall.
- In spring prune out any canes that look sickly.
- Don't water from overhead, and mulch generously to keep rain or hose water from splashing on leaves.

Botrytis:

Symptoms: this is a fungus that produces fuzzy grey mould. At first it looks like water marks on the leaves, stems, or even the flowers. In a few days, mould appears and that means anything affected is starting to rot. The saprophytic fungi can overwinter. And, alas, almost any plant can get this.

- It's a blight that often hits peonies. The new leaf shoots wilt when they are about one foot (30 centimetres) high. The spores can infect buds, flowers, leaves. The buds turn black. Cut all foliage to ground and get it out of the garden — not into the compost.
- As a last ditch effort, spray it with Bordeaux mixture (copper sulphate and lime) when the shoots hit about 10 inches (25 centimetres). Repeat at least twice. Lift any

infected crowns in the fall, dig out the rotted parts and dip the rest in the same Bordeaux mixture. Replant and give a good hit of compost.
- Make sure the plants have sufficient air circulation.
- Pick off infected leaves and get rid of them.
- If it continues, a good idea is to remove the top two inches (5 centimetres) of soil around the plant and replace it completely.

Mildew:

Symptoms: manifests itself in white powdery stuff on the leaves and shoots. It stunts growth.
- This could mean that the roots have dried out. I find this happens regularly with pulmonarias—I usually have them near ferns and hostas which grab the moisture—the leaves curl up when the roots are dry.
- Remove the affected leaves; give the plant a good soaking; then mulch with compost.
- Garlic is a natural fungicide; plant next to plants prone to this disease.
- Phlox seem particularly susceptible in the east—watch the lower leaves. Make sure they are in a sunny place with good air circulation.
- Spray milk on plants suffering from mildew or mould.

Rust:

Symptoms: comes in sienna-colored spores. Stunts growth. They can overwinter so clean up everything affected very carefully.
- Provide lots of space for each plant and keep the soil moist.
- Get rid of seriously infected plants.

Wilt:

Symptoms: Obvious wilting; first seen as leaves wilting; the fungi travel through the vascular system of the plant and plug it.

- Wilt often affects clematis. Injury from a lawn mower or from cultivating can cause the top to die back, but if there are no injuries it could be a fungal disease. Fungal disease produces reddish lesions around the stems which then proceed to wither away. Prune radically as soon as you notice the top growth going this way. Cut back to 6 inches (15 centimetres) above ground. Get rid of prunings safely.

Nematodes:

Symptoms: malformation of leaves, flowers, stems, die-back, yellow foliage. If you think that it's nematodes plaguing your plants, have the soil tested by a specialist (get names from your local Agriculture Canada office or see the list at the end of chapter 4 on *Bugs*). Take enough samples during a time of plant growth to make at least half a pint ($1/4$ litre).

Test on your own this way: take soil samples from different places in the garden at a depth of about 6 inches (15 centimetres). Mix them up and divide into six pots. Put three in the freezer for three or four days. Plant several fast-growing seeds such as radishes. Cover with peat moss and keep in a warm place to germinate. If the freezer soil is significantly better than the non-freezer soil, you probably have nematodes in the garden.

- If you have a very small garden, you can sterilize the soil by lifting the soil into containers and pouring boiling water over it.
- Plant marigolds which produce a chemical that bumps off the nematodes. Rotate marigolds with other plants from year to year. If you loathe marigolds, just snip off the flowers. This, by the way, is not a quick fix, and it might take a couple of years to inoculate the soil.
- Mustard plants, roots of asparagus, hairy indigo are all good cover crops to discourage nematodes.

• You can starve them out with immune or resistant plants.
    Don't be upset by the occasional appearance of a yellow
and curling leaf. Just keep on treating the soil with compost, manure and water.

CHAPTER SIX

WEEDS: FRIENDS OR FOES?

❧

NO MATTER HOW LONG I GARDEN, WEEDS CON-
tinue to stump me. I'm always so grateful to see
stuff come up in spring that I'm willing to let anything
grow. Then comes the shock of having to weed. I usually let
a plant grow until it's got a few leaves because I think I'll be
able to identify friend or foe. Ha! I usually forget; then it
means getting out weed identification books, but that
never seems to help. What I end up doing is going to the
messiest, most unkempt garden in the neighborhood. If
something's growing there, I probably don't want it in my
garden. I may lose a few flowers but not many.

Of course there are weeds I adore—the wild aster, for
instance, has a place in my garden as does Queen-Anne's
lace (which has the benefit of attracting parasitic wasps that
rid the garden of aphids), and a clump of goldenrod for fall
color.

My hortbuddy Amanda has started what she calls a
Railway Garden in front of her house. She cruises the
railway tracks and digs up appealing looking plants. It looks
a bit messy and some neighbors sniff at it. But I'll bet in a
few years everyone will like this rather enchanting bit of
wildness on a very domesticated street.

What's a weed? You could say it's any plant that's come
unbidden, and is invasive. By taking this view, you won't
be upset about a few weeds lurking about. I once tried
transplanting Queen-Anne's lace. No luck. But one year

it appeared on its own. The seed might have been dropped by a bird, or moved in by an insect.

Weeds don't grow everywhere but they do seem to thrive in places that are cultivated. This makes them less than wild in many cases. They are extremely well-adapted plants. Some weeds are actually herbs and very useful.

Weeds form an intricate community of plants. They can change the environment of your plants as their species change; and the kind of weeds will change as the environment changes. For instance, some weeds will increase seed production like wildfire if there is enough space between similar plants. Other weeds have, over millennia, come to imitate the crops they invade. There is a weed corn; a grass that looks like rice until it flowers; and lamb's-quarters will grow upright rather than prostrate just to fool you in the mint patch.

Not all weeds are natives and not all native plants are weeds by a long shot. Natives are the plants that have been here since Day One of plant history. Most weeds or the plants we consider weeds and therefore A Bad Thing are introductions—even if hundreds of years old. They were brought over by the first waves of Europeans in ships, on shoes, in pockets. Some by accident, some by design.

Weeds can be prodigious producers of seeds. Some put out hundreds of thousands per plant. And that's one of the reasons we're unhappy about them. They tend to take over everything else in their lust for survival. And many can wait for years, decades, even a hundred years, to germinate. So you never know when the little devils will spring up again.

What weeds might do is sap nutrients from the very plants you want to keep healthy. Some exude toxins from somewhere in the plant affecting the growth of flowers and shrubs nearby. This is called allelopathy. Other weeds may overwinter plant diseases and pests.

But all weeds aren't necessarily invasive, terrible things. They've been given a bum rap—many of them are very useful. Low mat-forming weeds can keep ground cool around vegetables, trees and shrubs. They can also hold nutrients in bare soil. Others attract beneficial insects or even act as trap crops. This makes it easy to hand-pick them. Really deep-rooted perennial weeds will break up hardpan that's as tough as concrete and draw nutrients that are deep in the soil to a much higher level. They can bring moisture to the surface under the most adverse conditions. The root systems of many weeds also provide channels for more domesticated plants. In other words, they can create the right conditions in which other plants will flourish. When they die, they provide the soil with fibre.

You can have weeds growing side-by-side with crops or flowers quite successfully. In many cases they make great companions. But there are a few caveats in this. You've got a problem if you have weeds such as bindweed and quackgrass—they will smother or choke everything around them. Bindweed roots are very deep and can put out runners 3 to 9 feet (1 to 3 metres) long. If you attack them at the root, you help them proliferate. Keep pulling the tops off until the root is starved and dies. Shallow-rooted weeds such as chickweed, on the other hand, will shade seedlings. Having a few weeds in bare spots will serve to hold in moisture, protect your plants and, most important, give bugs something to munch on.

One of the many reasons that weeds may move in on your territory is that your soil is not as fertile as it once was. Add lots of organic matter to improve the soil and help it get rid of the pest weeds that sap what nutrients are left.

HOW TO DEAL WITH WEEDS

- Clear a space for your plants and mulch them from 2 to 4 inches (5 to 10 centimetres).
- Place plants close together—the less space you leave bare the less likely weeds will invade—unless the plants won't like being moved when they reach maturity.
- Pull weeds until new plants are established, then weed every three or four weeks after that.
- Don't let annuals develop seed heads. Annual weeds, such as chickweed and lamb's-quarters, put out thousands of seeds from one plant. Cultivate the soil and mulch. If you're sure you've got a ton of weeds in one section of your garden, dig up the area, rake and then cover the surface with dark plastic. This will starve them of the light they need to germinate. If you are planting seeds or seedlings, make sure you mark them so you know which are friends. After each rain, get out there and pick away at the green stuff in between.
- Perennial weeds: pulling them out will encourage them—bindweed, for instance; or twitch grass—by tilling you'll help spread them. Use heavy layers of mulch if they are a real pain. Keep topping them off until the roots are starved.
- Keep mowing on a regular basis and cutting off tops until there's a killing frost.
- Cover crop: when I've made a new bed, I put in a creeping mint which helps keep bugs down and protects the soil.
- Weeds in the cracks: pour boiling water over them—it will help kill weeds and keep seeds from germinating. This really works well. I've managed to keep our brick walk clear without using herbicides
- If you've got weeds in your mulch or compost, try the following method to eliminate them: during the fall spread the material out on the ground, water and cover

with black plastic. They'll germinate and be killed off by frost and darkness.

- Cover the area with newspapers topped off with heavy mulch and just let it sit for a year.
- With many weeds such as thistles, wait until after a heavy rain and pull them out by the roots.
- When you are ridding yourself of poison ivy or poison oak—don't burn the remains (poison fumes) and be sure to wear protective clothing. Pull them out the minute you see that tell-tale three leaf formation. Remove whole plants in fall when they turn brilliant red. If any of this stuff gets on your body, wash it off with alcohol, water and a bit of chlorine bleach. Wash this off with an alkaline-based soap.

BENEFICIAL WEEDS

Weeds attract spiders which prey on insect pests. If you have space, leave a 3-foot (1-metre) strip of wild, un-disturbed vegetation. Spiders are a natural insect filter in the garden and will allow plants to flourish. They reduce leafhoppers, aphids, leafworm, spider mites. Some weeds stimulate the growth of valuable organisms in the soil and others exude poisons.

A = Annual; B = Biennial; P = Perennial

The good weeds:

Buttercup P: Retards growth of nitrogen bacteria; will kill off clover; but also discourages most other plants if you have something you want to get rid of.

Clover P: Plant clover instead of grass and you will add nitrogen to the soil; has beautiful scented flowers; a cover crop that is far easier to tend than grass.

Chickweed P: A herb rich in copper; eat it the same way you do cress.

Couchgrass P: Source of potassium for the compost; you can also mulch with it; don't let it go to seed.

Dandelion P: Beautiful deep roots that bring nutrients up from deep in the soil. If you want hardpan broken up, these plants will do the job. Tolerate a few and learn to appreciate the young leaves in salads. They cleanse the blood and improve the enamel on your teeth. Other flowers welcome them since they aid growth. Good for adding iron, copper to the compost. Makes an excellent liquid fertilizer for foliar feeding. Gather early in the morning and cover with water; bring to a boil; cool and strain. Dilute 1:4 with water, add a bit of liquid soap and blend.

Fleabane P: The oil from this plant repels mosquitoes and, presumably, fleas.

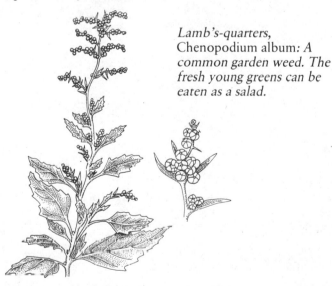

Lamb's-quarters, Chenopodium album: *A common garden weed. The fresh young greens can be eaten as a salad.*

Lamb's-quarters P: Aphids get trapped in these plants; host to lady bugs; indicates a nitrogen deficiency in the soil if they have a purply-red patina. You can eat them—good source of vitamin A. Adds strength to the following flowers: marigolds, peonies and pansies. This plant is high in iron, protein, Vitamins B1 and B2, and calcium. Allow it to grow near your tomato patch along with pigweed and sow thistle and you'll get a much better crop. They will also help plants withstand drought.

Purple loosestrife, Lythrum salicaria: *A garden perennial that in wetlands can choke out native vegetation.*

Lythrum salicaria, Purple Loosestrife P: Another European introduction, is a beauty of a plant. Alas, it has escaped into the wetlands cutting out the food supply that marsh birds depend on. And it's taking over the countryside. Once it's done a bunko into the wild, it really fits the category of weed. You must be very careful with it. Luckily for gardeners there are relatively safe hybrids. But you have to be able to trust that your nursery knows what it's doing. Look for *L.* 'Morden's Gleam', *L.* 'Morden Pink', *L.* 'Morden Rose'. Keep them deadheaded and away from wet areas. They are much too wonderful a plant to be ignored completely.

Milkweed P: Grows in dry soil; the juice from the plants cures warts—so they say. Traps cutworms for easy picking.

Mullein P: Another dramatic plant that can, if controlled, look good in the garden. You can get rid of it by cutting out the root below the crown. It indicates you have dry soil.

• Moth Mullein is particularly pretty.

Nettle P: False and stinging nettle. Pull out the roots or mow regularly. Use gloves when you're handling this plant.

• When young can be eaten in salads. Fends off slugs and snails. Excellent for the compost since it is a great activator and will speed things up if your heap seems a bit sluggish to heat up.

Ox-eye daisies P: I like these pretty plants. If you have too many, pull out by the roots right up to the fall. This will keep them under control and you'll be able to enjoy and cut the flowers.

Purslane P: They are really quite pretty with yellow flowers (they are a member of the portulaca family); use them in salads. If you have too many, pull them out. They only open when the sun is out. Don't put them in the compost.

WEEDS FOR EATING: • dandelion, milkweed, purslane, sheep sorrel, wild lettuce.

NASTY WEEDS

Annuals can generally be controlled by mulching from 2 to 4 inches (5 to 10 centimetres).

Bindweed P: Twining; beautiful but a real killer. Keep cutting it off—pulling up by the roots will just make it proliferate. It's going to take a few years to get rid of it. Hack away at anything that insinuates itself above ground.

Cocklebur A: Poisonous to some animals. Keep mowed.

Crabgrass A: Grows by stolons or creeping stems. Isn't crazy about good soil. So improve your soil.

Chickweed A: Seeds and creeps along. Keep pulling up and put in compost. Holds in too much moisture by not allowing a fair exchange between air and soil. It is edible when young.

Deadly Nightshade A: Attracts pests and diseases and will grow in the shade; keep pulling out.

Horse nettle P: Prevent seed formation, cover with sod.

Jimson-weed A: Poisonous narcotic, rich well-drained soil is its medium; cut back before it seeds, then get rid of all parts of the plant.

Knotweed A: Keep soil hoed and add manure. It may mean the soil is too compacted.

Plantain P: Usually a sign of compacting soil so aerate the soil. Add lots of compost or manure.

Quack-grass P: Rodale refers to this as a Jekyll-and-Hyde personality because it grows where nothing else will in the West; it binds loose soil and prevents erosion on slopes. But, and here's the Mr. Hyde part: it likes acid soil and increases by seed and underground stems (rhizomes). It grows fast, roots can travel 60 feet (20 metres) laterally and the seeds hang on so long it can choke out most other plants. Keep removing top growth, hack away at it with a sharp hoe.

• Spade up in fall and expose the rhizomes, then pull by hand. Leave a heavy mulch on top for a season.

Queen-Anne's lace, Daucus
carota: *A European biennial
now at home in fields
and along roadsides
throughout the
country. Also known
as wild carrot.*

Queen-Anne's lace B: This attractive plant can be a serious infestation since it's both hardy and spreads quickly. But I like it anyway and keep it confined to one plant, deadheading scrupulously; it does attract parasitic wasps which eat aphids.

Ragweed A: Don't get this plant mixed up with goldenrod. Ragweed is the one that affects those with hay fever. Keep it mowed close to the ground for control.

Smartweed A: This is a real spreader. Keep it mowed, drain if it's in a wet area.

Thistles P:
- Russian thistle should be cultivated or mowed down.
- Canada thistle must be dug out by the root—completely out—or it will start new plants. Good for the compost for potassium content. Cut right after pollination by removing blossom-heads and it will wilt. Don't let it flower.

109

Twitch grass: Tilling spreads it, so be very careful.

WEED INDICATORS

Plants act as indicators of what's going on in the soil they live in. Weeds are no different. They may indicate that your soil is exhausted, is becoming increasingly acidic, or lacks sufficient humus. When whole families of weeds move in it means there is a profound decline in the soil.

If you have any of the plants listed here, they may indicate the following kinds of soil.

Acid soil: cinquefoil, sheep sorrel, spurrey, swamp horsetail, dock, knapweed.

• For slightly acid soil: black-eyed susan, chickweed, daisy, yarrow. They could also mean that there is lack of air or poor drainage.

Alkaline soil: goldenrod, saltbush, saltwort.

Sandy soil: goldenrod, broom sedge, wild lettuce, onion, yellow toadflax, partridge pea.

Limestone soil: chamomile, pennycress, peppergrass, wormseed.

Rich soil: burdock, ground ivy, lamb's-quarters, pigweed, purslane, chickweed, buttercup, dandelions, nettles. All these weeds love to be in cultivated soil.

Poorly drained soil: bindweed, cutgrass, foxtailgrass, Joe-Pye weed, hedge nettle, horsetail, meadow pink, Saint-John's-wort, silverweed, smartweed, spiderwort.

Hardpan soil: chamomile, horse nettle, morning-glory, field mustard, pennycress, quack-grass, plantain. These weeds indicate that there is too much potash in the soil.

Ecological gardening means having a balance between what you pull out and what you leave in the world of weeds. Having weeds in the garden doesn't mean you are a lazy or sloppy gardener. Recognize the ones that are beneficial and keep them. Pull, mulch, chop at the rest. But don't put chemicals all over them.

CHAPTER SEVEN

PLANTING: COMPANIONS FOR LIFE

❧

OR A TERRIBLE PERIOD IN MY LIFE I DIDN'T HAVE control over my garden. I rented out the first floor of our duplex to people who swore they loved to garden. I watched as year after year my plants were swamped by what I referred to as those funny looking tomato plants: hemp, *cannabis sativa*, also known as marijuana. What I didn't know at this time of great despair was that this plant excretes certain pathogenic micro-organisms that were not destroying but protecting the other plants. They improve the health of the soil. I'm not in any way recommending that you plant these—they are illegal. It's by way of illustrating that plants perform the most astonishing functions. They have properties that we are just now beginning to recognize.

One of the major aspects of ecological gardening is planting properly—right plant, right place. A carved-in-stone rule is that you always put a plant in the area where its major needs will be met: a bog-loving plant in a damp area; a shade-loving plant in the right density of shade (light, deep, dappled or semi-shade). Then carry on trying all the suggestions set out below. The ecological gardener is going to be looking at wild roadside gardens, woods and meadows for inspiration. If you are ever in doubt about what you're doing in the garden, you can't go wrong echoing what you see growing naturally around you. When we get rid of the idea that we're here to dominate our environment and take on the responsibility of working with it, we'll bring Nature closer to ourselves.

There are many pluses to working in this way. Your garden will have much greater diversity in the kind and number of plants. Disease and insect problems will diminish when you achieve this in your garden.

COMPANION PLANTING

I never really believed in companion planting until the year Queen-Anne's lace appeared. One day I saw ladybugs on it and realized they loved this plant. From then on my garden has had at least one Queen-Anne's lace and a huge population of ladybugs. I learned more about this useful beautiful bug: they like daisies, butterfly weed, tansy, cosmos, fennel. In order to please, I planted them all.

The ancients, of course, found magical properties in herbs and many other plants. And we are just beginning to tap in on this rich source of information. After composting, the second biggest favor you can do your garden is put the right plants together. You can inoculate your soil, boost its health, aerate it by putting in certain plants. The perfect mix will include companions planted to protect one another by combining their environmental needs.

Companion planting can provide shade, protection from the wind, proper humidity, support or keep bugs and disease away. Instead of letting the plants compete with each other and have only the strongest survive, you can control this competition.

How to combine plants:
- Put sun lovers in front of those demanding less light. One can live very happily in the shade of the other.
- Put very deep-rooted plants next to ones with shallow roots.

- Plants with big roots can break up the soil for those with more shallow roots and bring up minerals from deep in the soil.
- Put plants that bloom early next to those that bloom later for a continuous display or crop.
- Put in heavy feeders first—they like lots of water and food—then follow later on with those requiring light feeding. Give them both lashings of compost. Peonies and delphiniums, for instance, are great gobblers but most herbs are light feeders.
- The same conditions of light and water make good companions.
- Don't crowd plants. If you're trying for an instant show, use annuals. Don't shove perennials up against each other. You'll only inhibit growth and future health.
- Give trees and shrubs lots of room but plant shade-loving shallow-rooted plants beneath them.
- Practise planting by allelopathy. Combine plants that exude certain oils from their roots to either inhibit or encourage the growth of other plants. Roots are always giving off some gases, their version of excrement.

Make the mix of plants mutually beneficial:
- Don't plant things together that attract the same insects and diseases.
- Aromatic plants that repel pests can protect those with little scent.
- Plant ones with early flowers that will provide pollen and nectar for some insect predators and parasitoids (insects that parasitize other insects), with plants that do not bear flowers until late in the season (or that are not allowed to flower).
- Plants that stimulate biological activity in the soil with crops that are heavy feeders.

Plants to attract bees:

You want bees in your garden because they will pollinate your flowers, thus making sure of their survival. Bees aren't necessarily attracted to scented flowers; and they love blue plants which often haven't any perfume.

- Wallflower, arabis, borage, all the campanulas, catmint, heather and heaths, thymes, honeysuckle, lavender, lemon balm, daphne, sunflower, asclepias, scabious, Michaelmas daisies or asters, roses, particularly rugosa roses, caryoptris.

Annuals: cleome, calendula, nasturtium, white alyssum.

Plants to attract butterflies:

Plants with nectar will attract butterflies. But they will plant eggs in herbs (dill and parsley), weeds (goldenrod, clover, milkweed, dandelions) and in willow or birch trees.

- Butterflies love yellow and purple blossoms; they don't like white roses.
- Flowers to attract butterflies: candytuft, mignonette, zinnias, phlox, portulaca, alyssum, wallflowers, sweet rocket and sweet William.
- Grow a butterfly bush, *Buddleia davidii.*

PROTECTIVE BOTANICALS

Now here's a real horticultural buzzword—botanicals. Plants and protective botanicals are plants that secrete an odor, or an oil from their roots which attracts or repels bugs or diseases. Don't expect an instant reaction however. Marigolds, for instance, discourage nematodes. But you might have to plant them a couple of years in a row to get results.

Trap plants: Many plants act as traps, that is, they attract an insect away from other plants so that it's easy to pick them off the trap plant.

- For instance, if you plant nasturtiums near tomato plants, aphids will be enticed away from the tomatoes to the nasturtiums.
- Mustard also attracts insects, so when they lay their eggs it's easy to destroy plant and eggs.
- Columbines attract spider mites.
- Milkweed can be used as a trap crop for cutworms.
- Herbs contribute mightily to the healthy garden. They protect plants from pests and disease and can be good fertilizers if you make a spray from their oils.

Repellents: Some plants are repellents rather than traps:
- Citronella is the most obvious—it keeps mosquitoes at bay; but there's also pennyroyal, the creeping mint; thyme, lavender, wintergreen, anise, bay, ginkgo, elder, pryrethrum.
- Mexican bean beetle is repelled by marigold, potato, rosemary, summer savory and petunia.
- Insecticidal flowers: asters, chrysanthemums, cosmos, coreopsis, nasturtiums, French and Mexican marigolds—plant them through the garden to discourage pests.

Some plants and their special properties:
- Anise and coriander germinate better if planted together.
- Bee balm, *Monarda*; planted with tomatoes, it really does improve their flavor.
- Birch excretes substances that encourage fermentation of compost and manure; place about 6 feet (2 metres) away.
- Borage contains potassium, calcium and other minerals and is an excellent companion for strawberries.
- Catnip, *Nepeta cataria*; use leaves steeped in water as a tea to keep flea beetle away.
- Chamomile, *Matricaria Chamomilla*; can be used against fleas; soak blossoms for two days; make a spray for diseases.

- Chives act as a fungicide. They keep roses healthy if planted nearby.
- Elder is a wonderful tree. It not only attracts birds, but also has other uses. Bruise the leaves and drag elder branches across a seed bed to discourage maggots.
- If you have horse-tail in your garden, don't despair. Make a spray: dry it; then cover with cold water; boil for 10 minutes. Cool and strain. Use 1:20 part water and spray. Or cut it down and use to scrub out pots and pans (this used to be a common practice).
- Dandelions absorb two to three times the amount of iron from soil as other plants. It's a natural humus producer and earthworms like them. The three-foot (one-metre) roots will bring minerals especially calcium, from beneath hardpan and deposit them closer to the surface. Earthworms use the root channels to go deeper into the soil; they exhale ethylene gas which encourages early maturity in nearby plants.
- Delphiniums contain alkaloids which can cause dermatitis; so do euphorbias.
- False Indigo, *Baptisia australis*, is repellent to chinch bugs, striped cucumber beetles; its powdered pods and seeds are toxic to Mexican bean beetle larvae. A sugar derivative from this plant is effective against chinch bugs, cotton aphids, squash bugs, tarnished plant bugs, potato leafhoppers, blister beetles, and spotted cucumber beetles.
- Fennel hates wormwood so don't plant them close together.
- Feverfew will discourage bugs if it's planted around your garden. I was first given a plant by Mary who always refers to them as "My father's little white flowers" and they've sprung up all over the place in a really pleasant way. Sometimes they are tucked under other plants. In light or shade they thrive.

117

- Plant flowering cabbage and kale with mint, thyme, rosemary, sage, hyssop.
- Four-o'clock, *Mirabilis Jalapa* has poisonous foliage but Japanese beetles love to eat them. The fact that they then kick the bucket doesn't seem to discourage them.
- Garlic deserves a section on its own. Not only is it a splendid food plant—fresh garlic is incomparable—it has many other uses as well. For instance, it keeps mice away from roses and lilies; planted near strawberries it keeps off nematodes and mould.

  Mince garlic in a food processor, mix with water and a little vegetable oil. This spray discourages insects and blights; and acts like an antibiotic on plants. Never plant garlic near gladioli—they don't like each other at all.
- Geraniums (pelargoniums—the hybrids you are used to seeing) are useful planted with roses since they'll discourage Japanese beetles.
- Have you grape vines? Then plant wild mustard to keep them healthy; bees love the flowers. Hyssop planted with grape vines will increase the crop.
- Hyssop, lemon balm and valerian are helpful to many vegetables.
- Lamb's-quarters planted near zinnias, marigolds, peonies or pansies will make them much more vigorous. It improves the soil. Plays host to lady beetle but is subject to leafminer (whose larvae the lady beetle loves).
- Larkspur, *Delphinium consolida*, is effective against aphids and thrips. Powdered roots are toxic to bean leaf roller, cross-striped cabbageworms, cabbage loopers and melonworms.
- Lovage inhibits the growth of nearby plants.
- Lupines add calcium to the soil; are valuable on poor sandy soil; plant near peonies, monkshood, elecampane, Michaelmas daisies, iris, daylilies, stocks.

- Marigolds, *Tagetes*; repels nematodes; useful with chrysanthemums, calendula, dahlias; around trees they will be protective because they have a big root system; plant under tomatoes as a soil covering.
- Nasturtiums need full sun but they do very well in poor soil. The addition of some potash aids blooms. Around apple trees they repel woolly aphids, cucumber beetles. Plant near broccoli to keep off aphids.
- Nettle is good in compost; helps plants withstand lice, slugs and snails; helps with growth of mint and tomatoes; will increase the scent of herbs.
- Parsley planted near bulbs, tomatoes and roses will protect them against black spot.
- Pennyroyal, *Mentha pulegium*, is supposed to repel pests in the garden and fleas from a cat's collar. I've planted it in my borders too recently to tell whether this will be effective or not. Some gardeners absolutely swear by it.
- Pepper juice inoculates plants against viruses borne by wind or bugs. Plant hot peppers to discourage insects.
- Petunias repel leafhoppers, so do geraniums.
- Pyrethrum, *Chrysanthemum coccineum*, is the natural source of many insecticides. Make your own by putting the flowers through a food processor and adding water. Strain and use as a spray.
- Rue, *Ruta graveolens* planted with roses will discourage Japanese beetle. Cats hate the scent so if they are tearing up the furniture, rub it on a cloth and drape over the favored area. Drives out fleas and flies; don't plant with basil.
- Salad burnet is rich in magnesium.
- Scotch broom accumulates calcium in the soil.
- Sheep sorrel takes up phosphorus.
- Tansy planted next to berry bushes will keep them happy.

- Wormwood, *Artemisia absinthium*, in a spray (boil up the leaves and strain) will discourage slugs on the ground; spray it around vulnerable vegetation in the fall; makes worms flee; protects against rust so plant near berries; will inhibit the growth of plants nearby.
- Yarrow grown next to herbs enhances their oils.

HERBS AS FERTILIZERS

Cut fresh herbs, put them in a bucket until half-full, and fill with water. Or use stinging-nettles if you have them in your garden or can cut them freshly in the country. Let sit and ferment. The mixture will smell a bit; when it gets strong enough, apply it as a foliar spray or near plants.

Roses:

- Plant herbs such as sage, lavender, thyme and hyssop near roses and they will keep out mice and slugs.
- Of course garlic will keep mice away as well as aphids.
- Plant parsley next to roses to keep off black spot.
- Plant Crown Imperial and lilies with roses as good companions to shade the feet of the lilies. They all have the same soil requirements. Crown Imperial, *Fritillaria*, has such a smelly bulb that it will discourage the mice and squirrels which are attracted to the lilies. It acts as a trap for lily beetles.
- Pot marigold, calendula and marigolds, if regularly deadheaded, will keep nematodes away from roses. If you suspect mineral deficiencies, correct by burying rusty nails around the roots of roses.

INDICATOR PLANTS

Plants give us lots of information if we know what to look for.

- Bachelor's-button, *Centaurea cyanus*, has blue blossoms when planted in limestone soil; rose and pink in acid soil. In fact, the redder they become, the more acidic you will find your soil.
- *Boltonia asteroides* popping up shows poor drainage.
- *Aster Tripolinum*, sea aster, indicates salt.
- Knotweed grows in acid soil and is rich in silica.
- Turn your *Hydrangea macrophylla* blue by adding aluminum sulphate to the soil. Dissolve ½ pound (250 g) in 5 gallons (20 litres) water. Do this once a week for 3 weeks then add 4 ounces (10 g) of ferrous sulphate. It will turn pink in non-acid soil. Add lime in fall.

INTERPLANTING

Here are more great tricks to help you mix your plants to their best advantage. Think of your garden in storeys: ground covers, low perennials, higher ones, small shrubs, big perennials and shrubs, and then trees. Remember, that though they grow slowly, for every foot a tree grows its shadow will cast another foot on the ground. Everything you add to the mix will change the environment—usually for the better.

Square foot planting:

One method of planting is the square-foot method. There is an entire book on the subject and if you've got a real space problem I recommend it (See Mel Bartholomew, *Square Foot Gardening*). Each square is planted with something different in blocks 4 by 4 feet (1.3 metres) square with an average of eight plants per square. You have little walk ways between each block so you never, ever step on the soil that you're cultivating.

RAISED BEDS

The biodynamic/French intensive method of planting uses raised beds. They increase the air supply to the roots. They will extend your planting time and plant range by at least a zone. It's also the best way to solve any problems you may have with poor drainage or crummy soil.

If you already have good soil, then making a raised bed is simple—just pile it higher than the soil around it (give it a bit of a slope on the edges). If you have poor soil and drainage:

- Dig down and lay a bed of rocks or junk left over from construction.
- Construct the sides of any material you like: railway ties, bricks, stones, almost anything that catches your fancy will do; just make sure that you'll be able to build a bed from 8 inches to 3 feet (20-90 centimetres) high behind it.
- Add a layer of gravel mixed with well-soaked peat. If you have compost add it as well.
- Top with good soil that's been well-raked.

CHART YOUR COMPANIONS

If you plant:	Accompany it with:
asparagus	tomatoes, parsley, basil
basil	tomatoes (dislikes rue; repels flies and mosquitoes)
bee balm	tomatoes (improves flavor)
borage	tomatoes (deters tomato worm); squash, strawberries
catnip	anywhere in border (discourages flea beetles)
chives	plant around fruit trees (keeps insects off)
garlic	roses, raspberries (enhances essential oils of herbs); use everywhere in the garden

hyssop	grapes; (deters potato beetle); (keep away from radishes)
lemon balm	throughout garden
marigold	throughout garden; keeps out nematodes, many insects
marjoram	throughout garden
mint	tomatoes
nasturtium	tomatoes, radishes; under fruit trees (enemy of aphids)
onion	strawberries, tomato, lettuce (against onslaught of slugs)
parsley	tomatoes, asparagus
petunia	throughout garden
pigweed	throughout garden (keep well-thinned, brings nutrients to topsoil)
pot marigold	tomatoes, (throughout garden for many pests)
radish	helps tomatoes, nasturtium (repels many pests)
rosemary	sage
rue	roses, raspberries (deters Japanese beetle); not near basil
sage	rosemary (keeps out some insects)
southernwood	here and there throughout the garden
strawberry	borage; lettuce
tansy	under fruit trees (deters pests of roses, raspberries, flying insects; Japanese beetle, ants)
tarragon	throughout garden
thyme	throughout garden
tomato	chives, onion, parsley, asparagus, marigold, nasturtium
valerian	anywhere
wormwood	keeps animals out
yarrow	enhances essential oils of herbs

Pest	Plant to repel
ants	pennyroyal, spearmint, southernwood
aphids	tansy
borer	garlic, tansy, onion
cutworm	tansy
eelworm	French and African marigolds
flea beetle	wormwood, mint, catnip
fruit tree moth	southernwood
gopher	castor bean
Japanese beetle	garlic, larkspur, tansy, rue, white geraniums
leafhopper	petunia, geranium
Mexican bean beetle	marigold, rosemary, summer savory, petunia
mice	spurge
mole	castor beans, mole plant (spurge), squill
nematode	African and French marigolds; salvia scarlet sage; dahlia, calendula or pot marigold, asparagus
plum curculio	garlic
rabbit	allium
rose chafer	geranium, petunia, onion
slug	prostrate rosemary, wormwood
squash bug	tansy, nasturtium
striped pumpkin beetle	nasturtium
tomato hornworm	borage, marigold, opal basil
white fly	nasturtium, marigold
wireworm	white mustard, buckwheat, woad

Source: *The Encylopedia of Organic Gardening*

CHAPTER EIGHT

WATER AND THE GARDEN

๙

A N ECOLOGICAL GARDEN IS EASY ON WATER. WE haven't unlimited supplies of this precious resource and some day, maybe sooner than we all imagine, we will have water rationing or be fined for leaving sprinklers running for hours.

There's a threat in my city that $40 will be tacked on to the water bill every time the lawn is watered. It's necessary to take all this seriously. In North America we are going through a desertification process swifter than in some parts of Africa. On the west coast around Los Angeles, the water table has been lowered by gross demand and this is terrifying.

There are a number of things you can do to preserve water: cut back on the amount of lawn you have as a start; use drought-tolerant plants, efficient watering systems and mulching (See Chapter 3, *Mulching and Fertilizing*).

We can't expect lush landscapes to be a right. This stress on the water supply demands much from the collective imagination. There are myriad things you can do with a little patch of land besides grow grass and some petunias. The possibilities are almost infinite in every region of the country—but first acquaint yourself with what you already have.

Try to imagine what the garden was like before all this cultivating, civilizing so-called, started. Think of how beautiful it must have been. We can no longer go back to that state, but we can try to understand the essence of those natural landscapes.

What vegetation is native to your area? What special light do you have? How far can you see—for miles or only up close?

WATERING AND YOUR SOIL

Know your soil—there's no point in following watering instructions for somebody else's soil. The root systems of plants fill out the air holes between the grains of soil. This is where the water goes, providing moisture and oxygen to the roots and the soil below. When a plant doesn't have the right amount of water, it becomes stressed, or goes into shock, and sometimes it's terminal.

So figure out what you've got in your garden and follow these general rules:

1. Water long enough for the water to go below the general root level. If you give plants frequent shallow waterings, you will encourage shallow root growth, which leaves them less likely to tolerate drought. It's better to water less often, more deeply.

2. Water plants individually if you can. This way you become sensitive to the needs of each of them.

3. Water early in the morning or late in the afternoon (more on this to come). Then carry on with how often and how much by considering the following:

Sandy soil: If you have sandy soil, the water runs through it very quickly. You can add humus to retain some moisture but it's still going to drain fast. You'll have to water more often, but you won't have to water for a long time.

• One inch (2.5 centimetres) of rain will penetrate two feet (60 centimetres). Sandy soil needs about two inches (5 centimetres) a week.

126

Loam: The perfect garden soil, enough humus to hold moisture in the soil, but good drainage. You should be so lucky.

• One inch (2.5 centimetres) of rain will penetrate 16 inches (40 centimetres). Needs about 1/2 to 3/4 inch (1 centimetre to 2 centimetres) a week.

Clay soil: The spaces between the soil particles are very close so water tends to move through it very slowly. You'll have to water for a long time, but not as often since it tends to hold water longer as well. Water slowly or it will run off in every direction.

• One inch of rain (2.5 centimetres) will penetrate 11 inches (28 centimetres). Needs about an inch (2.5 centimetres) a week.

All of the above, of course, depend on how hot it is, and the season. Keep an eye on your plants. Don't worry if they wilt and then recover at the end of the day. If they stay wilted over a 24-hour period, get out the hose.

Spring: hand-water transplants, seedlings

Summer: general watering

Fall: slow down once the days start to get shorter but be sure to water trees and shrubs well before frost sets in.

HOW TO WATER

At first, use a simple moisture meter to calculate how long it takes for water to reach deeply into the soil. It has been estimated that an inch of water (2.5 centimetres) will keep your soil moist from 5 to 15 days depending on your soil and the weather conditions. To achieve this same result takes one gallon (4 litres) of water per minute per 1000 square feet (93 m²) applied for approximately 10 to 11 hours.

Sprinkler system: If you use any of the twirling or revolving, looping back-and-forth systems, set out containers at different parts of the cycle to see how long it takes each to fill with 1 inch (2.5 centimetres) of water.

Drip irrigation: The most efficient water systems are drip. Hoses set on or in the soil water the roots rather than the surface. It's an abiding regret of mine that I didn't install a drip system when I redid my garden but someday when I tear it all apart, I'll make sure that this is the first thing I invest in. If you are starting a new garden, it is a good idea to figure out your watering method right at the beginning.

A simple method is to use an ordinary hose from the faucet to the edge of a drip system of feeder lines each irrigating about a 2-foot wide (60-centimetre) swath. You'll need them closer in sandy soil.

Custom watering: I usually water my plants by hand. I know this sounds as if I haven't anything else to do with my time, but I water as soon as the sun comes up—slowly, gently. It's a splendid way to start the day. I can also do a little slug slaughtering at the same time. For special plants I use a dipper, for the rest a hand-held hose with various nozzle selections: misting, for newly planted seeds; a fine spray for seedlings; a slightly heavy but soft rain quality spray for transplants. I have indicator plants spread around the garden. When one of them starts to look pathetic, I give it and the surrounding plants a good soak. Otherwise I leave them alone and hope that mulch and the weather will keep things cool and moist. I always have pails of water sitting around to get warm. Not all plants like cold water, certainly the little ones don't. I'm not much on cold showers so I assume plants aren't that crazy about them either. And there are a lot of plants, such as gentians, that can't cope with all the chemicals we have in city water. Let the water sit around and at least some of these chemicals, such as chlorine, will evaporate. When to water: Please, please don't water at night. It invites all sorts of bugs into that dampness and encourages mildew. Don't get confused between watering with a sprinkler and raining at night. The latter is going to be a different quality, more relentless, and bugs will be scurrying around to get away from it. Besides there's nothing you can do about it.

Remember that with the use of an oscillating sprinkler you'll lose at least 50 percent, though probably it will be closer to 80 percent, of the water to evaporation and wind. This increases the later in the day you water depending on how hot it is. Studies at American universities show that the optimum time to water is 5 a.m. If you can't make it out of bed that early, you can get inexpensive handy timers that attach to your water outlet to do it for you. The drawback is that they'll water whether it's needed or not.

Container gardening: The beautiful clay and terra cotta pots that look so good in the garden have one major drawback—they lose a lot of water. You will have to water at least once, if not twice a day. Ugly as they may be, plastic ones hold water much more efficiently.

PLANTING

Make sure you plant early enough and deeply enough that new plants get a chance to establish a long root system before the onset of hot weather. Use plenty of humus in the hole. This acts like a sponge to absorb water and distribute it to the root system in an even manner. Plant late in the afternoon and give them a good soak—never do this in the heat of midday. And give new plants a bit of shade for a week or so. Don't fertilize them too early in the season.

In very dry regions, add water retention materials such as Kitty Litter (clean please), which will absorb water and then release it during dry periods. There are also commercial water absorbents coming onto the market.

Perennials:
- Rule-of-thumb: they'll need an inch (2.5 centimetres) a week. By using humus or organic mulch, the temperature of the soil will stay cooler and require less water.
- Perennials that don't need a lot of water: fescues, junipers (the ground hugging type), coreopsis, asters, yarrows. Anything native to your area will also have adapted to drought.

Annuals:
- Annuals have shallower roots than most perennials.
- Annuals that don't require a lot of water: verbena, portulaca, salvia.

Shrubs:
- Once a plant is over two years old, you can hold back on watering unless it's looking poorly or wilted; then give it a good soak.

Trees:
- Trees take less water than shrubs. They send roots deep into the earth, drawing up moisture and aspirating it into the air around it—a kind of air conditioner. If you get a special attachment for your hose, you can deep-root water very effectively by driving it into the ground near the roots where the water will be used to its best advantage.

GREY WATER • Like many things in the horticultural world—the old ways are new again. Using grey water is exactly what my grandmother did when she threw the dishwater into her flower garden. The phosphates, even from low-phosphate soap, help plants grow lush foliage. Most flowers like it but acid-loving plants such as rhododendrons and azalea hate it. Be judicious. Studies in British Columbia have shown that plants watered with waste water yielded higher crops for vegetables—I can't attest to this, however, since I can grow so few vegetables in my small garden.

But check your local laws, especially if you decide to follow this practice at the cottage. Make sure you aren't aiming at a well. And if you are thinking of directing your automatic dishwasher residue into the garden, you'll have to refit the pipes. This may sound far-fetched at the moment, but suppose water rationing does comes into effect? Hmmm?

I came across a whole community of gardeners on Toronto Island. Every gardener had a form of cistern placed under the downspout from their roofs. It looked like something straight out of my prairie past. In those days no one, but no one, would have allowed a drop of rain to escape. A cistern trap is the easiest way to get water with little trouble. One inventive container was an abandoned electric soup tureen from a restaurant. It was large enough, had a spout for pouring off water, and a hinged double top.

LAWNS

Lawns are in this section because water is what lawns use most once they are established. I'm not a fan of grass. It's a difficult ground cover and I'm not wild about mowing. There's a place for lawns, but we've got to consider making them smaller, perhaps as only one element of the garden rather than the main feature. Use lawn as emphasis in your design—background for a woodland or meadow.

But if you still have grass, you've got to get it off chemicals if you have been using them. Any kind of artificial fertilizer will kill off the worm population (see *Chemicals* page 48) and they are crucial for the health of your lawn. Worse: if you've been using chemicals on your lawn, like all drug addicts, it will need, no, demand larger and larger quantities, and is much more likely to get a wider spectrum of disease and succumb to drought.

If you use a lawn service, don't let them apply chemicals and fertilizers automatically. Query them and make sure you have a choice. Lawns really don't need that much fertilizing in the first place and you're better off with an organic conditioner for the soil. Your lawn probably needs a fairly neutral soil (6.5 to 7.5). Test it with some litmus paper after a heavy rain.

Proper Mowing:
- No mower does a better job than a regular push mower. It cuts the grass (especially good are the ones with self-sharpening blades) rather than pulling or taking swipes at it as the gas jobs do. It will even do a better job than an electric mower. Always set the blade so it doesn't take off more than one quarter of the height of the grass. This may mean more frequent mowing but you probably need the exercise anyway. Keep it at a steady 2 to 3 inches (5 to 8 centimetres). The taller the grass, the denser the canopy. This will also kill off any low-growing weeds.
- Leave any clippings *in situ*—50 percent of the nitrogen will return to the soil. They will decompose faster than you expect and, since weeds need sun to germinate, it will help keep them at bay. That is, leave them if you're not using chemicals—in which case sweep them up and pitch them out in the garbage (not the compost). I recently heard a nurseryman on a phone-in radio show say that it was just fine to put grass clippings that had been sprayed with 2-4-D into the compost because it breaks down so quickly. Wrong, wrong, wrong. In all sorts of tests, it's

been found that even after a year of hot rot composting, 2-4-D is still evident. Don't use 2-4-D, but if you already have, don't put grass clippings covered with it in the compost unless it's very late in the season and you've only used it at the beginning of the season.

Proper Watering:

- Always water early in the day, just like all other perennials—the earlier the better.
- Water when the soil has become completely dry, probably not even once a week, to at least a depth of 1 inch (2.5 centimetres). If you have a good supply, water to 4 inches (10 centimetres).
- Light soils will drain more readily, so they will need more water and, by the same token, heavy clay soils will require less water.
- Don't water during a drought. The grass will go into dormancy and will come back once it has sufficient water. Consistent light watering will only encourage shallow roots that won't withstand any further dry conditions. The deeper the roots of your lawn, the healthier and tougher they'll be.

LAWN WEEDS, BUGS AND DISEASES

- The bug mostly likely to irritate your lawn is the chinch bug. Sabadilla dust or *Beauveria bassiana* are natural ways to control them.
- Diatamaceous Earth will control billbugs, nematodes and most other nasty bits of business.
- *Bacillus popilliae* will control Japanese beetle.

WEEDING • If you are plagued with weeds, increase fertilizing.

- Allowing the soil to dry out between waterings will inhibit weeds from germinating.
- Cut them out by hand and be sure to take all the root system at the same time.
- Chunks of yellow or dying bits of grass should be cut right out and re-seeded or sodded.

FEEDING THE LAWN

- Feed your lawn twice a year: spring and fall.
- Aerate in spring and fall by walking across it in crampons or golf shoes—actually there are spikes you can slip on over shoes that do the trick. This will also eliminate thatch—a layer of dead stems and roots that won't let anything penetrate.
- You can top dress with compost in early fall. Mix in grass seed for an extra thick cover.
- Organic nitrogen: this is the most important element your grass needs. Slow-releasing, non-burning nitrogen sources: fish meal, blood meal, hoof and horn meal, canola seed meal.
- Organic phosphorus: bone meal, SingleSuperPhosphate.
- Organic potassium: kelp meal and liquid seaweed; wood ashes (from the fireplace).
- Other natural amendments: calcium phosphate; sulphate of potash; sulphate of potash magnesia.
- Other organic fertilizers: sheep manure, bone meal (the coarse form is slower acting), cottonseed meal. Use in early spring and fall.
- Make pH adjustments in spring: use dolomitic lime to increase alkalinity.
- If grass looks on the yellow side, try blood meal, manure or cottonseed meal.

- Weak roots (lift out a chunk of grass and have a look at the roots): bonemeal or Phostrogen will add phosphorus and give them a boost.
- If you are seeding grass, use a mixture of seeds so that if one variety gets hit with a disease, the others can carry on.
- Use slow-release fertilizer—a low-analysis organic fertilizer. You don't want fast-release stuff on a shallow-rooted grass such as bluegrass. Thatch is likely to develop; it won't let water penetrate, therefore it will run off (along with the chemicals into the water table).
- If you have matted layers of root build-up—thatch—aerate the lawn and add some compost. There are heavy thatch rakes designed especially for this problem.
- If your grass looks diseased, it probably needs potassium. Try wood ashes.
- Slow-release fertilizers improve the health of your grass by creating humus. Humus acts as a sponge to hold nitrogen so the roots can utilize it.
- Enviro-Care is generally approved of by organic gardeners. But don't get sucked into the generic "natural." Read what the active ingredients are on the label.

Pesticides: Includes insecticides (bug killers) and herbicides (weed and disease destroyers).

- Look for ones that kill specific insects.
- Pyrethrum-based pesticides come from the chrysanthemum seed and are nontoxic to humans.
- Roundup: glyphosate—supposed to be safe because it attacks a gene in the plant and becomes inactive in the soil.
- Kleenup (Chevron, Ortho).

To dispose of any of these chemicals: buy only as much as you need at any time; get rid of them through hazardous waste or toxic taxis. Use them only as a last resort.

Lawn alternatives:

There is a sensible old rule about the soil: keep it covered because if you don't, the weeds will. Though grass has been regarded as the *ne plus ultra* of ground covers, it isn't really. You might think about other forms of ground cover. Green isn't the only beautiful color that nature has supplied us with. Look for the golds, tans and russets of native grasses, for instance.

Designer lawns:

- Clover: A lawn of clover strikes me as one of the loveliest. White or Dutch clover would be a good cover. White clover draws nitrogen from air into the soil and will improve it immeasurably.
- Thymes: I put in a front garden of assorted thymes. In a couple of years it turned into a tapestry that is pure pleasure to watch. Of course you can't do this if you've got acres to cover up. But if your space is manageable, try some of the following:
- A flowering lawn: This needs mowing, but only occasion-ally—usually at the end of June before dandelions and other sun-loving weeds get a head start. Set your blades about 3 inches (7.5 centimetres) high. Spring: Mow around the nicest clumps until plants go dormant.
- Winter aconite; snowdrops; hepatica (new leaf growth shows up after it blooms).
- Dutchman's britches, *Dicentra cucullaria*, spreads rapidly in a woodland venue—ferny foliage with tiny white flowers with yellow tips—plants go dormant in summer.
- Grape hyacinth, *Muscari*; daffodills.
- Plants that like a bit of shade and woodland conditions (high in humus, cool): *Claytonia virginica* and violets; rue anemone; wood anemone; bloodroot grows in woods as does the trout lily—a subtle beauty with an orchid-like flower. They spread by root shoots and will grow a patch

dense; wild ginger, *Asarum europaeum*, the European kind is smaller and shinier than the big *Asarum caudatum*, a native of British Columbia; Virginia bluebell, *Mertensia virginica*, partial shade; trilliums, *Trillium erectum*, purple trillium; woodland or wild blue phlox and of course *Viola labradorica*, an enchanting little violet and *V. tricolor*, the ubiquitous Johny-jump-up which will naturalize everywhere, especially in slightly acidic soil.

Summer:

- Blue-eyed grass, *Sisyrinchium montanum*, has a tiny blue flower in June.
- Firepink, Deptford pink, wild geranium, wild hyacinth and butterfly weed. Deptford pink blooms into September; wild geranium grows in open woods or sunny roadsides but tends to be patchy; milkweed attracts butterflies and can easily be controlled by mowing.
- Spiderwort or *Tradescantia* likes low rich soil and good sun.
- Crown vetch is extremely invasive and should only be used in areas where you can contain it. Has a pretty pealike flower. Excellent for controlling erosion.
- Evening primrose grows near dry sites; common primroses grow to 2 feet (60 centimetres).
- Yarrow, *Achillea millefolium*; let a clump bloom, then cut back.
- Moneywort, *Lysimachia terrestris*; Heal-all, *Prunella vulgaris*, a cone-shaped purple or violet flower that tolerates shade.

Fall:

- *Ceratostigma plumbaginoides*, dwarf plumbago or leadwort, is currently a big favorite of mine. It has brilliant blue flowers, turns crimson in fall and splits up easily for spreading.

- *Gaultheria cuneata* is evergreen and has white berries in autumn; aster, goldenrod; black-eyed Susan, *Rudbeckia hirta.*

Look at roadsides to see what grows best there. Identify plants using a good weed book and try out a section of your garden in this style. (For more ideas have a look at chapter 10, *Styles of Gardening.*)

XERISCAPING: TWENTY-FIRST CENTURY GARDENING

Xeriscaping is one of those new terms that is becoming a serious part of the horticultural lexicon. It's a concept that's been around since the early 1980s and I am sure it's going to become the norm. It abides by the principles of low-water landscaping.

- This is a way of gardening that uses drought-tolerant plants, or plants that have adapted to drier conditions, that fit in with the local environment.
- It uses plants indigenous to a region since they will withstand enormous weather swings much better than more fragile exotic plants. They will not suffer as much from insect damage or disease.
- It puts plants in the correct microclimate for them to flourish.

Start out by making a plan of your garden. Where are there good views? Do you have areas subject to erosion? soil poor? prevailing winds? A zone map will give you the climate zone you live in (examples in the chart at the end of this chapter show when frost comes in and out of some communities). Make yourself sensitive to the various microclimates in your garden. These will be influenced by the prevailing winds, the quality of shade, the number of hours of sunlight, how close to fences, the amount of light bouncing off a light-colored fence.

Water zones: Divide the garden into water zones first, and then decide what to plant where. For instance:
- perennials and small shrubs need a high water zone
- lawn would be moderate
- trees and large shrubs require the least amount of water so would be a low water zone

Then make a list of all the plants you have or would like to have and group them according to their water needs.

The concept behind xeriscaping is to group the plants with like water requirements together so you will waste the least. You will be echoing the natural system by planting lots of different varieties, by integrating vegetables with your flowers. You will consider your plants' root systems; how taller plants shade smaller ones; how the trees and shrubs are affecting the air quality. In other words you'll be much, much more aware of nature and its preservation.

The water zones also depend on the height of the land, the proximity to a water source, how far your hose system goes, the depth of humus in the soil, and the general quality of the soil you already possess. Use at least 4 inches (10 centimetres) of amendments such as manure and leaf mould. You will mulch of course (see Chapter 3, *Mulching and Fertilizing*).

- **Low water zone:** Use plants that have low water demands. They are very forgiving when a drought comes along. And these plants will probably be in the most exposed spots furthest away from the house.
- **High water zone:** Put plants that require the most water and attention within easy reach of the house. Because you'll be very conscious of the various microclimates in your garden, you can put the right plants in the right place—no one plant will overrun any other by being too successful.
- Plant so that tall plants will be on the north side of your design, and short plants on the sunnier south side.

- Remember that plants need lots of water at first. If they are watered properly, they will get along pretty well on their own after that.
- Use certain plants in separate parts of the garden as indicator plants; don't water until you see them wilt a little: once impatiens, artichokes, ligularia, ferns start wilting, water.
- Dig bigger holes for your plants and amend them with water-absorbing particles such as Water Grabber or Terra-Sorb; plant high in raised beds.
- Humus is necessary; it acts like a sponge absorbing and distributing water evenly and efficiently to plant roots.
- Since many new garden sites are low in organic matter, reserve precious compost for individual planting holes.

Water guzzling plants:
Perennials: bleeding heart, columbines, delphinium, foxglove.
Grass: Kentucky bluegrass.
Groundcovers: ajuga, baby's tears, myrtle, pachysandra.
Shrubs: azaleas, rhododendrons, yew, Japanese snowball tree, *Viburnum plicatum*, dogwood, *Cornus stolonifera*.
Trees: weeping willow, magnolia, trembling aspen, flowering dogwood, *Cornus florida*, red and sugar maples.

Whatever you do in the future, don't put in a water-hungry garden. These are referred to by environmentalists as hydroscapes. If everyone practised xeriscaping, water demand in your area could drop by about half. Keep this in mind: "As the greenhouse effect increases, we will see hydrological extremes," says James Hansen, Director of NASA's Godard Institute for Space Studies. "Some areas, especially mid-Continental regions, will have more frequent and extreme drought. At the other end of the spectrum, some areas will have extreme rainfall." Protecting our water is a responsibility for everyone.

EXAMPLES OF APPROXIMATE FROST-FREE PERIODS IN SOME SELECTED COMMUNITIES			
Area	Zone	Frost Out	Frost In
B.C. (north)	2 - 7	18 June	28 August
B.C. (Vancouver Island)	9	28 February	9 December
Alberta			
Calgary	3	28 May	September 9
Edmonton	3	14 May	14 September
Saskatchewan			
Regina	2	27 May	12 September
Manitoba			
Churchill	2	22 June	12 September
Winnipeg	3	25 May	21 September
Ontario			
Toronto	6	20 April	30 October
Quebec			
Montreal	5	5 May	7 October
Quebec City	4	18 May	18 September
New Brunswick			
Fredericton	5	18 May	26 September
Nova Scotia			
Halifax	6	15 May	15 October
Prince Edward Island			
Charlottetown	5	17 May	15 October
Newfoundland			
St. John's	5	3 June	12 October
Yukon			
Dawson City	2	26 May	27 August
Northwest Territories			
Yellowknife	2	30 May	16 September

Source: *The Encyclopedia of Organic Gardening*, 1978.
For information about your locality, or more detailed information, contact your nearest Agriculture Canada station.

CHAPTER NINE

OLD WIVES' LORE: WISDOM OR FOLLY

I N LATE SEPTEMBER HAVE YOU EVER OBSERVED A squirrel with a particularly bushy tail and thought, "It's going to be a cold winter." Well, if you have, you've been participating in an Old Wives' Tale: ancient lore based on observation and passed down through generations almost without examination. Most old wives' wisdom does have some basis though not about the squirrel's tail. What probably happened is that there was a cool summer and that's usually followed by a cold winter. So the squirrel would naturally have a fuller coat.

Take planting by the moon—now here's an old wives' tale that has real depth: transplant only with a waxing moon. The moon as we all know has a profound effect on the earth's magnetic field and that in turn modifies growth. It also influences the migration of water moving inside the smallest organism (much like it affects tides). Check this one out yourself—it's more likely to rain after a full or new moon. And this is precisely the weather you want after transplanting.

There is another bit of lore that advises you to plant in the buff. Since I do most of my gardening wearing not very much at all, I'd attest to that. But probably what the folklorists had in mind was that it should be warm enough so you could plant while naked.

In the 18th century they believed that you should never

plant the same thing in the same place twice. Now we call this crop rotation and of course it is the most sensible way to keep from depleting the soil. Except we now know that you shouldn't plant members of a family in the same place twice.

In earlier times, humankind's association was a more harmonious coexistence with nature. The game to be eaten was first praised, the peach or pear replanted. Nature was not "red in tooth and claw" but the great instructor. Nature was to be observed, to be learned from. In the ecological garden, we return to some of these practices. You can take this ancient wisdom with a grain of salt or you can fall in with old patterns of observing the moon's cycles while making your garden plans.

FACTS TO KNOW ABOUT THE SUN AND MOON

- The new moon waxes, or increases, until it becomes full then it wanes or decreases.
- The sun rises four minutes later each day. It travels through the entire zodiac, spending one month in each constellation.
- The moon spends three days in each constellation.
- Precipitation falls within three days of the new moon, so they say.
- It is usually dry at the midpoint of the waxing or waning moon.
- The moon is further from the sun in summer and winter. At its perigee (nearest point) to the earth plants will be vulnerable to pests and fungal diseases.

- An ascending moon fills plants with vitality.
- A descending moon will favor roots (good time for transplanting).
- When the horns of the crescent moon are sharply defined, there will be high winds.
- When they are dull, it will be humid.
- In fall, when the face of the moon is very sharp, expect frost.
- Since sap flow slows down during the ascending moon, this is a good time to prune.
- During a moon low on the horizon (autumn, winter) concentrate on composting, cutting, rooting, adding food to the soil.
- Harvest during a full moon for the best looking fruits and vegetables.
- A new moon will mean ants and sea animals are listless — watch what they are doing.
- Thunder as the moon changes means the weather will be moist.
- Pollinating insects have energy and vigor at night with the waxing moon, and are too tired to go about their business during the day.
- Pollinating insects have most energy during the day when the moon is in its first quarter.
- The nearer the moon's change is to midnight the fairer the weather will be for the next seven days.
- The nearer the moon's change to noon, the more foul the weather for the next week.
- Full moon at the equinox means violent storms followed by a dry spring.

ZODIAC		
Element	Sign	Influence on Plant Part
Earth	Taurus, Virgo Capricorn	development of roots
Water	Pisces, Cancer Scorpio	development of leaves
Light	Gemini, Libra Aquarius	development of leaves
Fire	Aries, Leo Sagittarius	development of fruit or seeds

PLANTING CYCLES

Once you've got decent soil, even in part of your garden, there are important decisions to be made about planting. If you work in harmony with nature you'll watch for the signs that tell you when is the best time. Here are some of the signs that guided the ancients:

- Plant annuals in increasing light: new moon to full moon.
- Plant biennials, perennials, bulbs and root plants in decreasing light: full moon to new moon.
- Never plant on Sunday—this day is ruled by the sun and is considered dry and barren.
- Don't plant on the first day of the new moon, or on days the moon changes quarters.
- The last quarter of the moon is best for preparing soil for cultivation.

February:

Aquarius—January 20 to February 19

- Airy, dry tendencies; barren and masculine characteristics. Don't plant during this sign.
- Indian legend: position of the moon during the first two weeks of February indicate whether the growing season will be wet or dry. If the horns of the moon point down the moon is emptying its water—be ready for a wet spring and summer.
- A dry moon with horns pointing up—plant early and use drought-resistant seeds.
- Prepare seeding-frames' soil early in February under Aquarius—dry or barren signs are best for turning sod.
- A new moon in Aquarius is a prediction that the crop will be poor because of blight or insects.
- If there was a full moon during February from the 1st to the 19th it was believed that the following summer's gardens would thrive.
- In February or March while the moon is passing through the moist sign of Pisces, cuttings should be planted in cold frames in rooting sand when moon is in 1st quarter.

March:

Pisces—February 19 to March 21

- This is a highly fruitful sign. Under Pisces, the moon emerges above the plane of the earth's orbit. When this happens it's good for planting (not in all parts of our country, of course). Pisces holds water and has feminine and productive characteristics.
- Best sign for starting seeds in a cold frame.
- Watery, fruitful, strong-rooted tendencies.
- Plants shoot up if seeded after March 21.
- First and second quarters of the moon are increasing phases—plants that produce yield above-ground should be planted.

- The third quarter is a decreasing phase during the dark of the moon. Root crops—carrots or turnips, for instance—should be planted during this period.
- The fourth quarter is said to be best for pulling weeds, cultivating and turning the sod.

April:
Aries—March 22 to April 20
- Fiery, dry, windy and barren characteristics. Never plant anything in the barren sign of Aries.
- Good sign for digging up the soil and pulling out offensive roots. Destroy noxious weeds and unwanted growth.
- Turn sod or plant posts especially during the last quarter of the moon or first three days of a new moon.
- Plants sown under the sign of Aries were believed to grow rank and full-leafed but wither before producing food and unlikely to hold fruit.
- In the first quarter: plant broccoli, barley, cabbage, corn, lettuce, chard, kale, endive, oats, rye, spinach and leafy vegetables.
- In the second quarter: plant beans, peas, squash and tomatoes.
- In the third quarter: plant beets, carrots, parsnips, potatoes, radishes, rutabagas, turnips, onions, bulbous flowering plants.
- The fourth quarter is bad for seeding. Prepare the soil instead.

May:
Taurus—April 20 to May 21
- Earthy, moist.
- A good time to plant since this is a productive sign.
- Taurus moon is hearty, and growing things respond with vigor if seeded at this time. They gain strength from the earthy influences.
- Avoid the first day of the new moon for planting.

- Plant leafy vegetables in the waxing Taurus moon.
- In the second quarter: replant snap beans, summer squash.
- Fertilize or side-dress with compost or mulch.
- Cultivate during the fourth quarter of the moon.

June:
Gemini—May 21 to June 20
- A sign of aridity and barrenness.
- Destroy weeds, trim, cut timber and build fence posts.
- Cultivate.

Cancer—June 21 to July 22
- Pregnant moon in June means enough rain to support a late crop.
- This is one of the most productive times for planting. You'll get a good crop and have a chance of plants maturing under Cancer.
- This is the time to finish planting the main garden.

July:
Cancer—June 21 to July 22
- This is a fruitful, watery, feminine sign.
- Fertilization of cucumber flowers by insects said to be affected by the moon: new sliver, the bugs rest at night and are vigorous by day.

August:
Leo—July 22 to August 23
- This is a lofty, firm, steadfast sign.
- The characteristics of Leo are fiery, dry, barren and masculine.
- Crops harvested under the characteristics of Leo will keep better for a longer time.

September:
Virgo—August 23 to September 23
- An earthy dry sign.

- Harvest root crops during the waning moon.

Libra—September 23 to October 23
- Moist semi-fruitful characteristics with airy masculine tendencies.
- Harvest in the third or fourth quarter.

October:
Libra—September 23 to October 23
- This is a moist sign.
- Harvest crops during the waning third or fourth quarter.
- Counteract the moist influences of Libra and any bruised spots will dry up.
- If you plant during the water sign of Pisces, it's logical that you harvest during the sign of Libra which is also a water sign and completes the cycle.

November:
Scorpio—October 23 to November 22
- This is a watery, fruitful, feminine sign.
- Best time to harvest apples.
- Mulch herbs.
- Slow to storm, slow to warm.
- Propagation of hardwoods is best done on the waxing moon: Take hardwood cuttings from all kinds of deciduous trees and shrubs as well as evergreens, yews, boxwood and hollies. Slips should be tied into bundles and kept in damp sand in a cool dark place.

December, January:
Sagittarius—November 22 to December 22
- This is a masculine sign, fiery, dry and barren.
- Slaughter meat during the waning moon.
- Graft while moon is passing through the fruitful watery signs of Cancer, Scorpio or Pisces, or earthy productive sign of Capricorn, or when specific days are ruled by those signs.

- Graft when moon is between new and full in the first and second quarters.
- Don't graft on Sunday.

Capricorn—December 22 to January 20
Aquarius—January 20 to February 19

- Cut under Capricorn and hold to Aquarius.
- Radically prune grapes during the second quarter of Capricorn—if pruned on the swelling moon, grapes will grow round and juicy.

WEATHER

A pleasant aspect of ecological gardening is being in tune with the universe. You become a weather watcher, sensitive to changes in the moon, cloud formations and the direction of the wind. Weather affects all our senses dramatically. Most of us who garden are almost subconsciously aware of this, but it is satisfying to be a little better informed. The ancient wisdom and lore have a lot to tell us. A few weather facts:

- Rain and lightning are fertilizing agents. When lightning hits the ground, nitrogen charges into it (250,000 tons produced each day in 1800 storms).
- Sulphur comes with rain.
- Snow has nitrogen, phosphorus and other minerals (really helps the crops in the north).
- Fog contains iodine, nitrogen, chlorine.
- Dust restores minerals to exhausted soil and contains bacteria.
- An attractor of static electricity (a metal pole) will increase the size of tomato plants.
- From three a.m. until noon, sap rises, and from 3 p.m. until midnight, the lower parts of plants are influenced by

the revolution of the earth. Therefore, harvest leafy vegetables in the morning and root crops in the afternoon.
- Falling barometric pressure which precedes a storm means that the atmospheric pressure on your body falls, less oxygen is rushing around in your body and you feel sluggish.
- Good weather means high barometric pressure, therefore less humidity, more energy, better feeling all around.

SOME ANCIENT WEATHER PROPHECIES • Dew needs a clear sky and a windless night. A cloud cover holds heat and won't allow the drop in temperature required for condensation. When night breezes move warm air over the ground, they prevent the formation of dew. Morning dew embodies the conditions for fair weather.

> *When the dew is on the grass,*
> *Rain will never come to pass.*

and the opposite:

> *When grass is dry at morning light*
> *Look for rain before the night.*

Fog forms on windless cloudless nights. But in winter it is the result of warmer, wet air blown over cold land surfaces.

> *A summer fog for fair,*
> *A winter fog for rain;*
> *A fact most everywhere,*
> *In valley and on plain.*

Winter

> *Clear moon*
> *Frost soon.*

Night Time Weather

> *Cold is the night*
> *When stars shine bright.*

Foul Weather

> *A pale moon doth rain*
> *Large halo round the moon,*
> *Heavy rains very soon.*

Or:

> *Sound travelling far and wide,*
> *A stormy day will betide.*

Smoke that goes to ground rather than rising will indicate that there's a storm brewing—the air pressure is dropping.

> *When the wind is in the East,*
> *'Tis neither good for man nor beast.*

Or:

> *Winter thunder, summer hunger.*

Of course if you grow sempervivums (hen-and-chickens) on your roof, you will keep lightning from striking it. And witches will avoid your house.

Fair Weather

> *Red moon doth blow;*
> *White moon neither rain nor snow.*

Or:

> *When the bees crowd out of their hive,*
> *The weather makes it good to be alive.*

SOME PLANT OBSERVATIONS FROM OLD WIVES AND HUSBANDS •

- Sow early peas for rabbits, broadcast lettuce to fool the birds, cabbage plants to satisfy early butterflies.
- Transplant when leaves of the sugar maple, lilac and cottonwood flip over to show their light undersides.
- When barn swallows are really striking out for mosquitoes it means that their wings are weighted down in heavy air. The soil will be moist.
- In the East: cabbage flies finish laying eggs when the dogwood trees bloom; wait to set out brassicas and they won't be bothered by root maggots.
- Chard and beets planted after the lilacs have bloomed won't be bothered by leaf miners.
- When waterfowl seem to be flying high it means the air pressure is lowering and bothering their sensitive ears.
- Increased air pressure is likely to make animals restless.
- When a storm is coming, sap rushes to plants' roots to prepare them for the onslaught. It rushes back to the branches and leaves to repair any damage when it's over.
- Chickweed, dandelion and daisies close up when air pressure drops.

Though we can all learn from the sayings of the past, of course, being gardeners, we apply common sense to our gardening and work with the microclimate our garden provides.

CHAPTER TEN

STYLES OF GARDENING

❧

A GARDEN OVERLOADED WITH EXOTICS, STRAINING against its surroundings, is not only poor design, but will probably not survive. The great landscape designers of our time are looking toward ornamental grasses rather than lawns; they no longer sneer at native plants as too coarse or vulgar. And they've stopped imitating English and European formal designs. Gardening in North America has come into its own.

All kinds of gardening from vegetable to herb to perennial is a form of partnership with nature. If you adjust your style of gardening to the kind of soil and weather conditions of your region, you will be able to practise effective gardening. Thus you avoid the nonsense you see in Southern California. This is desert country but people insist on green, green grass, swimming pools, fountains and lush plants. They have changed the water table but this hasn't yet discouraged them from wasting water. And most of the rest of us participate in this kind of profligacy. One of the saddest photographs I've seen recently is the one of an Angeleno spray-painting the dead stuff outside his house a vivid green.

Imagine, for instance, that these people were living with the land instead of on top of it. They'd be developing beautiful desert and drought gardens that would enhance the landscape. The sanest way to garden is with the microclimate you've got. Gardening isn't necessarily some form of wish-fulfilment or self-indulgence. Enhancing what you find is one of the important functions of a gardener. Our responsibility as gardeners is to leave things better than we find them.

THE NATURAL GARDEN

You can't just clunk Meadow-in-a-can seeds all over the front garden. You might, if the bed is prepared carefully, get a rather glorious show the first year. But the next year, only the strongest will survive. And each year—unless you tend it carefully—you'll end up with a field of one aggressive plant. Probably goldenrod.

A natural garden takes careful thought. You must be familiar with plant communities: what lives well with what. It can take many forms: woodland or meadow, or a contained wilderness if that isn't a contradiction in terms, or a miniature prairie. Once a natural garden is mature, it will probably require much less maintenance than a conventional garden.

A natural garden doesn't have to have only native plants. What you want is *any* kind of plant that has adapted to your terrain, and to the amount of water you can afford to give it. For instance, hybrid tea roses are tricky creatures, fussy, demanding, but *rugosas* and shrub roses are tough and very hardy. Switch. Don't look for sexy or trendy hybrids, look for the simplest forms. Anything that is closest to the species form is the one for you.

Natural design has to be just as careful as any other. Choose a balanced mix between flowers, grasses, even weeds. Don't chop everything down but leave those with dramatic seedheads to enjoy all through the winter. Use the understorey of trees and shrubs for woodland plants echoing the wild. Nature is the inspiration you turn to for planning as well as for the plants you choose.

In the politically correct garden you'll want something that captures the essence of a natural plant community. You don't really want a meadow in the back 40 feet, nor a complete prairie habitat in a small front garden. What you want is the *feel* of it, an aspect of its soul.

What you also don't want is some dirty great useless landscape that doesn't fulfil any function except to look green. Which it won't, if we go through more and more dry periods as greenhouse effect experts warn us.

- If you must have lawn, choose grasses that are extremely hardy to your area.
- Find plants that adapt well to your climate if they are not natives.
- Learn which native plants thrive best and introduce them to your landscape. Use non-indigenous plants if they are well-adapted to climate conditions similar to your own.
- Try to use plants that have more than one function. For instance, any plants in the pea family fix nitrogen in the soil; many edible herbs provide both subtle beauty and a haven for bees; perhaps a beautiful ground cover will also be excellent for stopping erosion.
- Choose a wide variety of plant families so that nothing can wipe you out if a disease happens to come your way.
- If you look to hybrids, make sure they've been improved in the right way—not for double blooms, frills and freakish size—but for hardiness, drought-resistance, scent.

These plant lists are only suggestions because each region across the country differs and suitable plants will depend on your hardiness zone, the altitude you live at, prevailing winds and availability of water.

GROUND COVER ALTERNATIVES

If you do decide to give up your lawn, you will probably want to replace it with some other form of ground cover — to help protect the soil, hold back erosion and provide great beauty. Don't think that a ground cover has to be a very low plant. They can go as high as a couple of feet (60 centimetres). You can be as unconventional as you want. Perhaps you'd like to see a whole lot of one of my favorites: plumbago, *Ceratostigma plumbaginoides*. It has three seasons of color: stunning blue flowers that go on for weeks and scarlet leaves in fall.

For damp places: mosses are hard to start but great once they take root. Bog rosemary for a slightly acid damp soil. For shade: *Epimedium alpinum*; wild ginger; bugleweed; periwinkle, *Astilbe chinensis* 'Pumila'; deadnettle, *Lamium maculatum* 'Sissinghurst White'; or *L.m.* 'White Nancy'; one of my all-time favorite plants is Lady's-mantle, *Alchemilla vulgaris*, which does as well in sun as it does in shade — it's so flexible I use it as an edging plant wherever I can.

Primroses all like rich soil with some shade. Any of the lungworts; foamflower, *Tiarella* is a sea of white flowers in the spring plus it has the added advantage of attractive foliage.

For sunny places: woolly thyme (this one loves the warmth of rocks); crown vetch; pussy-toes, *Antennaria dioica* 'rosea'; chamomile; creeping Jenny or moneywort, *Lysimachia nummularia* is a very pretty but invasive plant with brilliant yellow flowers in spring; another beauty is Irish Moss, *Arenaria verna* 'Aurea'; any of the sedums make splendid ground covers and most are very hardy; sweet William, *Dianthus barbatus*; maiden pink, *D. deltoides*; wild sweet William, *Phlox maculata*; moss-pink, *P. subulata*, and creeping phlox, *P. stolonifera* all have an honored place in my garden.

GARDENING WHERE IT'S DRY

A really dry garden will have poor soil, probably quite sandy, and you will have to build it up with as much organic matter as possible. The soil will drain very swiftly. Therefore this is the situation where you hit the street and gather up everyone else's unwanted leaves.

The Dry Garden:

- Think of the silver plants—most of them like sun and have adapted very well to little water.
- Succulents, such as sedums and sempervivums, conserve water in their thick fleshy leaves.
- Shrubs and ground covers that tolerate drought: semi-arid shrubs; aspen, ninebark, Buffalo berry, sweet mock-orange, mahonia, potentillas.
- Grasses: crested wheatgrass, buffalo grass, Canada bluegrass.
- Ground covers: penstemon, woolly thyme, blue veronica, Greek yarrow, hardy pink, rock soapwort.
- Dry perennials: santolina, basket-of-gold, creeping phlox, white yarrow, ox-eye daisies, coneflowers, penstemon, Iceland poppy, gaillardia, yucca, evening primrose, prickly pear.
- Herbs: creeping thyme, woolly thyme, lemon thyme, golden marjoram, oregano, lavender, santolina, yarrow, sage, creeping mahonia, chamomile.

Surely this is one garden where the lawn is totally out of place. Look away from the lush greens to the tawny tones, subtle colors and lots of movement. I love Mediterranean plants in the dry part of my garden: I have as many different kinds of lavender as I can collect. They come up at different times and a couple keep flowering right to the end of October. If you are in a zone that's warm enough try rosemary—in my zone six, I grow different varieties of rosemary plants in big terra cotta pots to keep a touch of the Mediterranean. It does mean that they have to be brought in during the winter. If I lived in a warmer zone, I'd grow citrus plants, lily-of-the-Nile and, certainly, bougainvillea.

The Desert Garden: Look for plants suited to the hottest, driest places. Again think first of the silver foliage plants: sagebrush, *Artemisia tridentata* has beautiful leaves in summer but they are dry in winter; prickly pear, *Opuntia*; hawthorn, silver-leafed buffalo-berry.

Keep an eye out for red spider mites. Mottling of leaves will be an indication. Spray plants with water and try to make a direct hit on any webs that develop.

When planting, add a fistful of oats or barley to ferment and produce heat for the newly forming roots.

Desert accents: Succulents (echeveria, aloe, agave, sedum and euphorbia), rosemary, thyme, purple alyssum and sea lavender.

Prairie Garden: The prairie garden is a dry meadow garden. Use herbaceous rather than woody plants. These are plants that disappear into the soil when they become dormant and reappear the following spring thus avoiding the ravages of winter winds. They need at least six hours of sunshine. To ensure that you have the right mix, you will be better off removing a bit of your lawn or present garden at a time and planting islands of plants. As usual, make it a mixture of annuals and perennials Any prairie meadow should include some grasses and a combination of flowers.

Flowering time is summer and early autumn rather than spring; remember this when you are choosing your plants.

- Flowers for a dry prairie garden could include sea holly, purple coneflower; asters—there are dozens native to each part of the country; purple-flowering gayfeather; prairie coneflower; compass plant; bluestem grass; false indigo; prairie coreopsis.
- Trees: maple, beech, birch, sumach and aspen.

A Meadow Garden: You can't go wrong with black-eyed Susan, butterfly weed, wild ginger, crested iris, sweet Ciceley, bee balm, California poppy. Look for domesticated species of wild plants.

Japanese Garden: If you decide to try and create a Japanese garden, please, please don't think that putting in a few rocks, raking some gravel flat and adding a couple of plants alongside a Japanese statue or lantern is going to make a garden. The Japanese have a long, exceedingly complicated history bound up in their gardens and the placement of every rock is significant. One of the easiest, most foolproof things to start with is a dry stream bed—collect smooth stones and arrange them in the garden so they are either a feature or the focus of your design. The essence of the Japanese garden is simplicity and elegance—no clutter, a place for contemplation. Dwarf evergreens look appropriate in this setting. If you are interested in bonsai, you now have a place for these dwarf plants. Try the following: Japanese black pine, *Pinus Thunbergiana*; azalea; creeping lilyturf, *Liriope spicata*—good for both sun and shade; *Camellia japonica*; mondo grass, *Ophiopogon japonicus*; blue fescue; Irish moss, *Arenaria verna*; heavenly bamboo; yew. Lily-of-the-Nile in large pots in colder regions looks stunning; in warmer areas grow them directly in the garden.

Oasis Planting: Plan a dry garden around one area and direct water to another for an oasis. Feed and care for the oasis separately from the other. For the oasis you'll need mulch and rich soil. The further you get from edibles the less water the plants require (the true cottage gardens of old had the vegetable and cutting garden close to the house where water was available and the ornamentals further away).

Edibles: nut and fruit trees, fig, grape, Jerusalem artichoke, mulberry, olive, persimmon; and herbs, such as thyme, oregano, rosemary and marjoram.

GARDENING WHERE IT'S WET

Wetlands: If you have wetlands instead of a formal water garden why not let it be as natural as possible—perhaps extend a well-designed platform or bridge into it. Alas, what you don't plant here any more is the flashy and gorgeous *Lythrum salicaria*. It's just too dangerous in boggy or wet ground because it will take over. Even the hybrids should be avoided in this situation.

Plants: Ferns; hostas; *Rodgersia aesculifolia; Iris sibirica*; cattails; lotus and water lilies; buttonbush, *Cephalanthus occidentalis*; red-osier dogwood, Cornus sericea; and bamboo.

The Seaside Garden: Grasses: These will do very well in wet soil: eulalia grass; silver feather grass; paper plant, *Cyperus papyrus*; feather reed grass; maiden grass; zebra grass; drooping sedge; Gray's sedge; corkscrew rush; Japanese sweet flag; manna grass; silver spike grass. For a ground cover *Rosa rugosa* will tolerate salt spray very well.

Woodland Garden: Natives include: rue anemone; trillium; trout lily; spring beauty, *Claytonia*; Toothwort, *Dentaria*.

GARDENING WHERE IT'S COLD

The northern garden has special qualities: Long, long summer days for quick growing compensate for protracted winters. Look for plants that are listed in seed and nursery catalogues as being completely hardy. Lots of hardy shrubs will survive winter kill right down to the ground and come round again in the spring.

- Be sure to water all evergreens heavily before the onslaught of the first freeze-up. If trees and shrubs have to go through a winter without heavy-duty watering before freeze-up, they are likely to be affected by sun and wind damage.
- Usually northern gardens have a deep and consistent snow cover to help them through the winter. But make sure branches aren't overloaded with snow and ice or that ice hasn't accumulated at the base of plants.
- Plan the garden around the color of trees and shrubs when they are not in bloom, since winter is around for such a long time.
- Ground covers: Arctic phlox, *Phlox borealis*; clematis, *Clematis tangutica*; Japanese spurge; kinikinick; snow-in-summer, *Cerastium tomentosum*; sedums; Virginia creeper.

SELF-SOWING GARDEN

One of the easiest gardens, certainly one that will sit lightly on the land, is a self-sowing garden. It's almost impossible to imitate such perfect informal drifts. Move any volunteer seedlings around once you learn how to identify them and stick them in the right place. I like to leave a couple of places in the garden where nature can take its own course and usually it looks marvellous.

Be sure to deadhead all summer long and then let selected plants go completely brown and dry. The wind, birds and your movement in the garden will sow the seed. I shake the seeds where I want them. Just don't let strong volunteers crowd out or starve weaker plants. Mark where these plants are or you'll dig them up in the spring. On the other hand, they may surprise you and that's always a welcome quality in the garden.

Encourage growth among paving stones and stone walls if you're lucky enough to have either. All around the Mediterranean wherever you see a wall, you'll find Red Valerian, *Centranthus Ruber* ; (not the awful spiky annual). It has enchanted me since the first time I saw it. Keep on deadheading and it'll keep coming back.

One of my favorite self-seeders is one I brought back from Salt Spring Island many years ago. It's rose campion, *Lychnis Coronaria.* It's been happy in my and most of my friends' gardens ever since. It's a great plant with wonderful grey foliage and brilliant magenta flowers that keeps on blooming practically to death—good cutting plant too. If you find the color too strong, keep the flowers cut so that you can appreciate the extravagant silver foliage.

Amanda has forget-me-nots all over her garden and now they're in mine. Wallflowers; snapdragons, *Antirrhinum*; mulleins; foxgloves are all great self-seeders.

One of my all-time heroes, Christopher Lloyd, recommends Mexican daisy, *Erigeron karvinskianus* (Zone 9); and spurge, *Euphorbia stricta.*

Remember that if you have hybrids they won't come true from seed. That means you won't get exactly what you planted the first time and the results might be dreary or something quite fascinating. I have some candytuft that self-seeds and each year it changes color: now it's heading for whites and pinks instead of the original lilac.

One columbine that I let go to seed has turned around several times, has become smaller and sometimes has more interesting colors. I deadhead anything dull, then take the

ones I particularly like and isolate them just to see what will
come up next year.

Fall planting of self-seeders:

You can fall plant the following and not worry about
them. I never remembered where I'd put things so I eventually got smart and now I mark the areas.

Amaranthus; California poppy, *Escholozia californica*;
China asters, *Callistephus chinensis*; cleome; corn cockle,
Agrostemma; cornflower, *Centaurea cyanus*; cosmos;
datura; delphinium; echium; forget-me-not, *Cynoglossum*;
gaillardia; hollyhock, *Alcea*; love-in-a-mist, *Nigella*; mignonette, *Reseda odorata*; nicotiana; pinks, *Dianthus*; annual poppies; portulaca; sage, *Salvia*; salpiglossis; silene;
snapdragons; snow-on-the-mountain, *Euphorbia marginata*; stock and sunflowers.

Sow in fall just the way you would in spring or let the
flowers themselves set seed (just don't deadhead or pick
them all).

Annuals	Height	Color
California Poppy	12"-24" (30 cm-60 cm)	yellow to orange
Candytuft	16" (40 cm)	many colors
Cornflower	12"-48" (30 cm-120 cm)	white, pink, blue
Cosmos	36"-72" (90 cm-180 cm)	white, pink, red
Forget-me-not	12"-24" (30 cm-60 cm)	blue
Love-in-the-mist	18"-24" (45 cm-60 cm)	blue, white
Marigolds	4"-24" (10 cm-60 cm)	yellow, red
Nasturtium	7"-24" (18 cm-60 cm)	yellow to orange to red
Pot marigold	12"-24" (30 cm-60 cm)	yellow to orange
Statice	24" (60 cm)	yellow, lavender
Sweet alyssum	3"-12" (8 cm-30 cm)	white to violet
Zinnia	12"-30" (30 cm-75 cm)	many colors

Perennials	Height	Hardi-ness Zone	Month of Bloom	Color
Candytuft, *Iberis sempervirens*	12" (30 cm)	3	April-May	white
English Daisy, *Bellis perennis*	6" (15 cm)	3	April-June	white, pink, purple
Feverfew, *Chrysanthemum parthenium*	12"-36" (30 cm-90 cm)	4	July-August	white
Foxglove, *Digitalis*	36" (90 cm)	4	June-July	white to purple
Golden Marguerite, *Anthemis tinctoria*	36" (90 cm)	3	July-August	yellow
Lupine, *Lupinus*	1'-8' (30 cm-240 cm)	3-6	June	many colors
Mountain Bluet, *Centaurea montana*	24" (60 cm)	2-3	May-July	blue
Penstemon, *Penstemon barbatus*	3'-6' (90 cm-180 cm)	2-3	June-August	red
Sweet violets, *Viola odorata*	8" (20 cm)	6	April, May	violet to white
Biennials				
Dame's rocket, *Hesperis matronalis*	3'-4' (90 cm-120 cm)	2-3	July-August	white, purple
Holly hocks, *Alcea rosea*	9' (270 cm)	2-3	July-September	many colors

Honesty, *Lunaria annua*	36" (90 cm)	8	July- September	white, purple
Moth Mullein, *Verbascum blattaria*	36"-48" (90 cm- 120 cm)	3	June- September	white and pink
Evening-primrose, *Oenothera biennis*	36"-48" (90 cm- 120 cm)	4	July- September	yellow
Sundrops, *O. fruticosa*	24"-36" (60 cm-90 cm)	4	July- September	yellow

Herbs:

Borage, *Borago officinalis*, annual, to 30" (75 cm)

Catnip, *Nepata cataria*, 36" (90 cm), zone 3

Chamomile, *Chamaemelum noile* 12" (30 cm), zone 4, August-frost

Chervil, *Anthriscus*, annual, 18" (45 cm)

Dill, *Anethum graveolens*, annual, to 48" (120 cm)

Hyssop, *Hyssopus*, 18" (45 cm), zones 2-3

Marjorum, *Origanum majorana*, annual, 24" (60 cm)

Salad burnet, *Sanguisorba officinalis*, 5' (150 cm), zone 4

Summer savory, *Satureia hortensis*, annual, to 18" (45 cm)

Tansy, *Tanacetum*, 36" (90 cm), zone 3

ENDANGERED BULBS

Bulbs make wonderful garden additions. They aren't only for spring, there are also great bulbs for the summer garden. But serious problems have emerged. Some bulbs have been collected in the wild in such profligate amounts for decades that they've managed to make it to the endangered species list. If you are fond of the following plants, please get them from other collectors or from seed exchanges and hold off buying them from nurseries. That is, until you can be assured that they have actually been cultivated under nursery conditions. Apparently many of them are collected in the wild, then repackaged as a nursery-grown product. The Dutch bulb growers are going to be designating wild collected. Many of the more responsible nurseries are waiting until there are nursery-grown stocks to sell to their customers. It's better to go that route.

- *Anemone blanda, Arisaema, Cardiocrinum giganteum, Cyclamen* (but not *C. persicum*), Cypripedium, Dracunculus, Eranthis cilicica, E. hyemalis, Galanthus (but not *G. nivalis,* snowdrop), *Iris acutiloba, I. sibirica elegantissima, I. paradoxa, I. persica, I. tuberosa, Leucojum aestivum, L. vernum, Narcissus asturiensis, N. bulbocodium conspicuus, N. bulbocodium* 'Tenuifolius', *N. cyclamineus, N. juncifolius, N. rupicola, N. scaberulus, N. triandrus albus, N. triandrus concolor, Pancratium maritimum, Sternbergia* spp, *Trillium* spp, *Urginea maritima, Uvularia.*

PLANTING BY INDICATORS

Indicator plants are those plants that give you information about the conditions in your garden. I have a couple of indicator plants in each part of my garden. If they flop about looking wilted, I water. I don't bother if they seem to be able to take it. There are lots of ways to use indicators and I've tried to mention them in each chapter where it's relevant.

CHAPTER ELEVEN

FINALE

❧

IF YOU WANT TO LIVE IN YOUR GARDEN IN HARMONY with others, you'll have to let the children in. I don't know what I did that was wrong but none of my children have grown up to be gardeners. Maybe they are so casual about it because they were lucky enough to have had a garden at their disposal. They claim if they had something terrible to tell me, they'd lure me into the garden and we'd sit and talk about it. I'd become so distracted pulling out weeds that whatever they had to say became much less intense.

I haven't any grandchildren of my own yet, but I do have Andrew and Mack who live next door. From the time they were old enough to sit up they've come over the fence to visit. In this complicated garden with checkerboard squares, woodland, cutting garden, they've never broken or messed up a plant. To them it's an enchanted space. They've put in dozens of bulbs, planted popsicle sticks, collected pine cones from the country for mulch, gathered stones to make a dry stream. The garden is very much theirs as well as mine. But of course the minute they get hyper I send them home. You can't do that with your own children so here are a few suggestions:

- Make a patch of garden that is strictly theirs and keep out. This can be a shady part for a fort (nothing fancy— old boxes will do); or a vegetable garden. Just as long as it's a secret place and very personal. An old unconventional bunk bed set became in turn a fort, a ship, bridges. When my kids finally gave up on it, it was left on the front walk and taken up by other kids on the street.

- A space in a shrub became a secret hut. A weeping mulberry is good for this.
- Most kids love digging—let them help. They'll discover that worms aren't yucky in the hand, that lots of bugs are not scary but fascinating. Teach them which are friends.
- Show them how to live with insects but make some rules. For instance, never swat at a sucking bee; don't touch certain plants that might be poisonous; don't pick up any bug they don't recognize. However, don't overload children with too many rules—it will ruin the pleasure of the garden. If they make mistakes and you lose a few plants it isn't a disaster. Include them in the gardening chores that are most fun:
- Watering with a nice long wand and gentle spray.
- Planting seeds that are guaranteed to have spectacular results: scarlet runner beans, pumpkin, sunflower. If they can end up eating whatever they plant, it's even more successful. It will also make the connection between the soil and their food, something they won't get in a supermarket.
- Placing stones for a walk. I found this really effective. I let Andrew put rocks or bricks all through the front garden at the right intervals for his three-year-old legs. He's extremely proprietorial about the space and I like watching him and his friends hopping about. They are very careful.
- Cleaning up interesting tools.
- Helping to cut plants back.
- Making a mulch mix—leaf mould, peat, manure; or helping mix up manure tea.
- Allowing them to get dirty.

Animals are rather more truculent. My cat, Mickie, deems the entire garden to be her own. She doesn't walk on plants, well, not most of the time. But she's perfectly willing to lower her bulk on them and sleep. For some reason, a beautiful *Erica carnea* is her favorite roost. The only thing that will keep her away from plants that succumb to this kind of treatment is to put in little pointed sticks around them. I keep herding her into corners under shrubs or overhanging plants where she can be cool and non-destructive.

- Dogs: again you've got to leave a spot for them to have on their own. You can set up minimal barriers and hope that by planting as intensively as possible you will discourage them from running about the garden, but they are trainable, unlike most of their owners.

By not making the garden too sacrosanct a place, by giving it the feeling of an extension to the house, by making it useful as well as beautiful, the garden can become a valuable teaching tool as well as a sanctuary.

THE CHRISTMAS TREE DILEMMA

Here's the dilemma: you don't really want to buy a plastic confection but can't bear the thought of chopping down another tree. Don't feel guilty. Some trees are bred to be harvested as in Christmas tree farms. Make sure yours comes from one and not from the wild. You are recycling the tree when you chop it up and use it as mulch and for protectors around shrubs.

You can recycle the tree in many ways:

- Tie the whole thing, or just branches, to the fence and use bits of popcorn, cookies and fruit on it for birds.
- Put the branches in window boxes; add dried berries and seed pods.
- Use branch tips for sachets or potpourri; use large branches as mulch.
- Wire wide branches over trellised vines to protect them from drying out.

- Chop large branches into mulch for acid loving plants.
- Dry the trunk for firewood or garden stakes.
- Not a tree, but save cardboard cylinders from wrapping paper to make collars for young plants to protect them 'from cutworms.

But if this still isn't the route you want to take, try the following recommended by Ron Kelly at The Arboretum at the University of Guelph. Buy a small conifer (less than 5 feet/2 metres) in a five-gallon (20-litre) pail or in peat to keep the root ball in place during the relocation process. Prune in early fall after shoot growth is over and before new growth starts. Mulch around the tree. Dig a hole where you want to put the tree after Christmas; fill it with leaves. Put the soil in a place where it won't freeze. Bring the tree inside as close to Christmas as possible. Make sure it isn't near either heat or light sources. Two weeks later— no more—return it to the garden. Moisten first with warm water when you dig it in. Put leaves around as a mulch.

JOINING THE GRASSROOTS MOVEMENT

A few years ago on our street we found we were gathering more and more often in little groups to talk over our concerns about the environment. We'd all been listening to Dr. David Suzuki's radio series *It's A Matter of Survival.* We were terrified by the information. We also knew that, like many people who live in this city, we hibernate once winter settles in. Action was definitely needed.

A few hardy souls put out a notice inviting everyone on the street to come to a meeting. About ten people showed up; several more sent notes saying they were interested. Within a few months, we were a really solid group calling ourselves Grassroots Albany (because Albany's the name of the street). We decided after a lot of discussion what projects we wanted to take on. We covered everything: fine paper recycling; getting more trees planted on the street; buying only recycled paper products (by buying in bulk for the street we got great deals). We shared recycling information with each other; found out which merchants in the neighborhood were environmentally responsible; wrote letters to politicians, and to big and little businesses. And we got to know each other.

But our main thrust was to act as a lobby group. And this, we decided, is our job: to get as many people involved as possible—on a street to street basis. A way to keep in touch, to give a sense that it's possible for each person to make a difference. We sent out our little kit with letters, the Grassroots logo and all the information we'd gathered. We asked anyone who got in touch with us (about 1000 at this writing have done so) to copy all the material ten times and get it out to ten other neighborhoods or groups.

We meet on the second Tuesday of every month at precisely 8 p.m. and pack it in at 10. At least that's when the recording secretary stops recording. Of course we carry on. Sometimes to have a glass of wine, sometimes to discuss matters until much later.

A week before the next meeting the minutes are distributed to the group. Just how many show up is elastic. Sometimes there are eight, sometimes there are twenty people. And always there are at least a couple of observers who want to start their own group.

We've found this an ideal forum for people who wouldn't necessarily march, or banner-wave, or make a fuss. It's small enough that everyone has projects to work on, large enough that no one has to feel guilty if they don't get everything done they promised to do. Guilt is precisely what we don't need.

Since we've been doing this a long time, there is always a member who can go on a panel, attend a conference, make a presentation—with passion and intelligence. It's given us all a much greater sense of being in control of our own lives in a small way. We've all become good friends.

Here's our logo and anyone who wants to organize a Grassroots neighborhood group is welcome to use it; we've translated it to T-shirts; bags for our own use; and again we're sharing them with anyone who wants them. The following is the kit we send out to interested people: *When there's a Grassroots group on every block, in every school, in every office, we'll change the world, give it back its future.* Remember: environ-

mentalism makes sense—it isn't kookie or anti-industry or unrealistic. It recognises the necessary limits to our planet's resources. It tries to minimize our destructive impact on air, water, and the earth-support systems all life depends on. Environmentalism is everybody's business.

THE GRASSROOTS NETWORK

By working together, individuals can have a dramatic impact.

Here's How:

1. Start where you already belong in the community—at work, at school, at your club, on your street.

2. Find like-minded souls—one or two—talk over the idea of forming an action group, and set a date for a meeting.

3. Let everyone who might be interested know—conversation, a note, a simple sign on trees and lamp-posts.

4. You'll end up with a core group of committed people, and others who'll come and go. Your aim is to spread the message: *each individual really does make a difference.*

5. Start simply. Find out how you'll operate as a group. What are your goals? Do you want a group project—clean air or water, saving the wilderness—local or national? Or will you support each other with individual projects? What will you do about recycling, reducing garbage and carbon emissions?

6. You'll learn from meeting—don't burden yourselves with rules. People often stop coming because they haven't done what they'd promised. Remember there's always another meeting, another chance to get it done. Major changes evolve.

7. We've found it works best to schedule meetings on the same night every month—the second Tuesday for instance suits us.

What Happens: We've been learning how to live more environmentally benign lives, how to take action on issues that really concern us. We've written a lot of letters, called a lot of people, planted a lot of trees, and had fun. We've thought what it means to become a group, to listen to each other. And we've helped many other groups get started. It's been good for us and our neighborhood, as well as for the environment.

Letter writing: When most people write letters of complaint, they go on too long or sound like cranks. We should encourage people to write, write, write to the following:

large companies
politicians at every level
small businesses who carry over-packaged products
fast food outlets
restaurant chains

How to Become a Lobby: Lobbyists know that what makes a difference is having numbers on their side. Keep in mind that as one person you're a voice crying in the wilderness, but as three or three hundred you are on your way to becoming a lobby. Politicians and Chief Executive Officers do have people who read for them.

- They pay much more attention to letters than to pre-addressed cards.
- They pay more attention to a letter that is succinct, calm, rational and on one page.
- Don't insult the addressee even if you feel impassioned to do so. The reader will quite rightly stop reading.
- To show your concern, try to write your letters on recycled paper if it's available.

The letters below are meant to be guides rather than form letters. They don't have to be typewritten, legible handwriting can be even more effective. Just don't send out a photocopied form letter; they tend to be dismissed.

- Never keep your fears to yourself, now is the time to speak up. Hit people at all levels—local politicians, small and large businesses, giant multinationals. Fast food chains produce more garbage than almost any other business. You might want to tackle them. Until we stop feeling impotent against these forces and become one voice telling them about our concerns, they will not make changes.
- Personal and passionate can make a difference.

Chief Executive Officer or President
(*call the company and get the correct name and spelling*)
Address

Dear M-----:
We are told over and over that the packaging of your products is consumer-driven. If that is indeed true, I should inform you that I no longer buy the following of your products. I feel they are so overpackaged that they are a serious danger to our environment:(list the products perhaps with description [i.e., the cream in a tube in a plastic bubble tacked on to cardboard; the hamburger in paper in plastic in plasticized bag].

Until you come up with a more streamlined, environmentally friendly form of packaging (I suggest you look back to the 30s and 40s to see how it was done), I will find alternatives. I'm willing to do without this product or pay more if I feel it will help this crippled planet.

Your name, address and date

Politician's name
Address

Dear M-----:
My family of 00 voters has passed the stage of being angry about the relationship between your government and the environment. We are terrified. We live in a city where our children are being poisoned, where it is more important to have [domed stadia or whatever other aberration upsets you] than it is to have clean water. We are appalled at the misplacing of values when all about us, we're convinced, our planet is strangling to death because of untrammelled growth.

Can you possibly understand this fear? Pl
the following sites to discover why we care
[*put in the problem that bothers you in a sentence or
two*].

It is our intention not to vote for any politician or
party that does not have a real and demonstrated interest in the environment first. Development for development's sake, quick and easy profits and promises of
jobs are no longer good enough.
More in anger than in sorrow,

Name, address and date

Sample to a large company, such as a pulp and paper
company

Dear M-----:

I am living in a state of fear about the rapid decline in
the health of our planet. You say you only harvest our
forests but I've seen what clear-cutting can do and it
will not reproduce itself in my or my children's lifetime
and in some areas such as Vancouver Island, never. A
few jobs, profits for a few people, are no longer acceptable when our world is so threatened.

It is time that your company took the environment
seriously. Surely you too have children, and grandchildren that you care about. Do you want them to
drink poisoned water and breathe fouled air?

Responses: If you get no responses, organize your group
to write again with a further letter along the more in anger
than sorrow line. If enough people co-operate, we can run a

177

list of large companies, businesses of all kinds and politicians at every level who are indifferent to our pleas.

Fine Paper Recycling:

Do recycle: bond paper—cannot usually be colored kind but the basic office clean stuff;

computer paper even if it's been typed on;

ledger paper;

cardboard and manila envelopes, broken and bundled, flattened.

Keep all these categories bundled, bagged, or boxed separately.

Don't try and recycle:

anything with staples, paperclips;

glossy material;

window envelopes;

tapes.

How to become more environmentally friendly at home: Use reusable shopping bags, containers (string, canvas, bundle buggy, cardboard box) to save bringing home plastic bags.

Segregate your garbage into organic matter, packaging, recyclable containers, reusable containers and products. See what the various piles are made up of and try to find ways to reduce them.

Shop against packaging. Buy in bulk (taking along your own store of empty containers, reusable paper and plastic bags). Remove excess packaging at the checkout counter, explaining in a brief and friendly way why you are doing this.

Start composting organic matter.

Recycle properly in the blue box, if your community has a curbside recycling program.

Don't purchase anything that's environmentally unfriendly (e.g. carry your own reusable coffee mug with you instead of using a styrofoam one; don't buy large plastic garbage bags, plastic wrap or baggies, etc).

Use only recycled paper.

Reuse as many yoghurt pots, margarine containers, etc. as you can. These will soon be recyclable through the blue box program.

Switch to environmentally friendly household cleaners which you either purchase or make yourself.

Use rags instead of paper towels, cloth napkins instead of paper, toilet tissue and sanitary products made of recycled materials.

Be aware of the source of the foods you buy and avoid those whose production endangers the environment either through pesticide use or destruction of rainforests for agricultural purposes. Buy as much as possible seasonally and try switching to organically grown produce— balance costs by serving more meatless meals.

Shop locally: they're more likely to stock the brands and bulk products you want; you may also be able to influence store practices that infringe on the environment.

Explore energy-saving products such as rechargeable batteries and full spectrum fluorescent bulbs.

Return to the old days as far as energy use is concerned— turn off lights, etc. When purchasing appliances consider their energy consumption.

Use a bike or walk if possible.

Use public transport.

Only use unleaded gas.

In Grassroots Albany, we've found some encouraging and some discouraging things that only serious re-education is going to address.

By putting a container that looks somewhat like an enormous blue mayonnaise jar on an obvious front porch, we've got almost everyone dropping off paper for recycling. Another household takes glossy magazines to be used in schools or distributes them wherever else they might be needed. Members have started composting programs in the local schools. In fact, the little kids are much more aware of environmental issues than many of their elders. When we tried to have more trees, free trees, planted on the street, many people turned us down. Why? Trees are dirty and they didn't want to be bothered cleaning up all those leaves. Since the air-scrubbing quality of trees is fundamental to survival and the quality of air in the city, you wonder what planet these people have been living on.

Perhaps one of the things we should be pushing for is nature education starting in grade one and continuing to high school.

We found it easier to get the city to stop spraying our local park with chemicals. Yes, they are still spraying, even in the places where the children play.

But other good things have happened: we're all dedicated composters and have spread that news all over the area. Master composter Amanda gives annual updates; we had a display at the Smithsonian's Earth Day symposium in Washington; started recycling projects in every member's workplace. We've talked to schools, professional groups, on radio and television.

If you do form a group, please get in touch and tell us about it: *Grassroots Albany, 211 Albany Avenue, Toronto, Ontario M5R 3C7 Canada*

Remember the words of the immortal Pogo:
"We have seen the enemy—and it is us."

APPENDIX

PLANT LIST

The common names of plants have been used throughout this book, though this can be confusing. It's much safer to use botanical names. When precision is called for, I've put the Latin names after the common names. Here are the botanical names of many of the plants mentioned if they were not already given in the main text. There are annuals; perennials (spp after the name of a plant means species); biennials; trees, shrubs and ground covers.

Common Name	Latin Name
alyssum	*Alyssum*
alyssum, sweet	*Lobularia*
asparagus	*Asparagus*
aster, blue wood	*Aster cordifolius*
bachelor's-button	*Centaurea Cyanus*
basil	*Ocimum Basilicum*
bay	*Laurus*
bee balm	*Monarda didyma*
bindweed	*Convolvulus*
borage	*Borago*
broom, Scotch	*Cytisus scoparius*
burnet, garden	*Poterium Sanguisorba*
butterfly bush	*Buddleia*
calendula	*Calendula officinalis*
California Poppy	*Eschscholzia californica*
candytuft	*Iberis amara; I. sempervirens; I. umbellata*
castor-bean	*Ricinus communis*
catmint	*Nepeta*
catnip	*Nepeta cataria*
chamomile, sweet	*Matricaria recutita*

chervil	*Anthriscus Cerefolium*
chickweed	*Cerastium*
chives	*Allium Schoenoprasum*
chrysanthemum	*Chrysanthemum*
cleome	*Cleome*
cornflower	*Centaurea Cyanus*
coreopsis	*Coreopsis*
cosmos	*Cosmos*
daffodil	*Narcissus*
daisy, English	*Bellis perennis*
daisy, Michaelmas	*Aster laevis*
dandelion	*Taraxacum*
daphne	*Daphne*
daylily	*Hemerocallis*
dill	*Anethum graveolens*
false indigo	*Baptisia*
feverfew	*Chrysanthemum Parthenium*
forget-me-not	*Myosotis*
four-o'clock	*Mirabilis Jalapa*
foxglove	*Digitalis*
garlic	*Allium sativum*
geranium	*Geranium*
heather	*Calluna*
hollyhock	*Alcea*
honesty	*Lunaria annua*
honeysuckle	*Lonicera*
horsetail	*Equisetum*
hyacinth	*Hyacinthus*
hyssop	*Hyssopus*
kale	*Brassica oleracea*
lamb's-quarters	*Chenopodium album*
larkspur	*Consolida*
lavender	*Lavandula*
lemon-balm	*Melissa officinalis*
lovage	*Levisticum officinale*
love-in-the-mist	*Nigella damascena*
lupine	*Lupinus*
Marguerite, golden	*Anthemis tinctoria*
marigold	*Tagetes*
marigold, pot	*Calendula officinalis*
marjoram	*Origanum*
mignonette	*Reseda*
mint	*Mentha*
morning glory	*Ipomoea*

mountain bluet	*Centaurea montana*
mullein	*Verbascum* spp
nasturtium	*Tropaeolum*
onion	*Allium*
parsley	*Petroselinum crispum*
pennyroyal	*Mentha pulegium*
penstemon	*Penstemon* spp
petunia	*Petunia*
phlox	*Phlox*
pigweed	*Amaranthus hybridus*
pyrethrum	*Chrysanthemum coccineum*
radish	*Raphanus sativus*
rocket	*Hesperis*
rosemary	*Rosmarinus officinalis*
roses	*Rosa*
rue	*Ruta*
sage	*Salvia*
savory, summer	*Satureja hortensis*
sorrel, sheep	*Rumex Acetosella*
southernwood	*Artemisia Abrotanum*
spurge	*Euphorbia*
squill	*Scilla*
statice	*Limonium*
stock	*Matthiola*
strawberry	*Fragaria*
sundrops	*Oenothera fruticosa*
sun plant	*Portulaca grandiflora*
sweet William	*Dianthus barbatus*
tansy	*Tanacetum*
tarragon	*Artemisia Dracunculus*
thyme	*Thymus*
tomato	*Lycopersicon*
valerian	*Valeriana*
violets, sweet	*Viola odorato*
wallflower	*Cheiranthus Cheiri*
wormwood	*Artemisia*
yarrow	*Achillea*
zinnia	*Zinnia*

ORGANIC AMENDING

Material (rapid, medium slow release)	N	P	K
blood meal (r)	15	1.3	.7
bone meal (s)	4	21	.2
cattle manure (m)	2	1.8	2.2
cottonseed meal (s-m)	7	2.5	1.5
dried blood (m-r)	12-15	3.	-
fish emulsion (m-r)	5	2	2
granite dust (s)		5	
leaf mould (composted m)	.6	.2	.4
mushroom compost (m)	.4-.7	57-62	.5-1.5
oak leaves (r)	.8	.4	.2
phosphate rock (vs)		30-32	
sawdust (vs)	4	2	4
seaweed (s-m)	1.7	.8	5
wood ashes (r)		1.5	7

SOIL TYPES

	look	feel
Clay	cracked crusty, shiny like plastic when wet	hard when dry sticky when wet forms large lumps
Sandy	loose, porous won't hold shape	easy to work dries fast
Loam	full of crumbs spongy	easy to work well-drained aerated

SOIL AMENDING METHODS

Clay	lots of organic matter lime to improve texture green manure dig up in fall to overwinter
Sandy	organic material with peat moss compost leaf mould
Loam	keep the nutrient level up with organic material

ORGANIZATIONS

These organizations all have excellent journals that are received with membership.

Canadian Organic Growers
COG Membership Secretary
P.O. Box 6408, Station J
Ottawa, Ont. K2A 3Y6
$16.00

Wildflower Society
75 Ternhill Crescent
North York, Ont. M3C 2E4
$20.00

Ontario Rock Garden Society
c/o Andrew Osyany, Box 146
Shelburne, Ont. L0N 1S0
$15.00

If you want to support a group that is working towards building a sane and sustainable agriculture in North America, send your donation to:

Ecological Agriculture Projects
P. O. Box 191, Macdonald College
21, 111 Lakeshore Road
Ste-Anne de Bellevue, Que. H9X 1C0

BIBLIOGRAPHY

Andrews, Brian. *Northern Gardens*. Edmonton: Lone Pine Publishing, 1987

Appelhof, Mary. *Worms Eat My Garbage*. Kalamazoo, Mich.: Flower Press, 1982

Ball, Jeff. *Rodale's Garden Problem Solver: Vegetables, Fruits, and Herbs*. Emmaus, Pa.: Rodale Press, 1988

Bartholomew, Mel. *Square Foot Gardening*. Emmaus, Pa.: Rodale Press, 1981

Boland, Bridget and Maureen Boland. *Complete Old Wives' Lore for Gardeners*. London: Bodley Head, 1976

Bonar, Ann. *The Garden Plant Survival Manual*. London: Quill, 1984

Bremness, Leslie. *The Complete Book of Herbs*. Montreal: Reader's Digest Association, Montreal, 1989

Buther, Gerald W., Edward Jackson and Richard Sudell. *Simplified Gardening*. London: Ernest Benn Limited.

Campbell, Stu. *Let It Rot!: The Gardener's Guide to Composting*. Pownal, Vermont: Garden Way Publishing, 1975

Cox, Jeff. "The Pacific Northwest" in *Organic Gardening* (July/August 1990): 26

Druse, Ken. *The Natural Garden*. New York: Clarkson N. Potter, Inc., 1989

Foster, Catharine Osgood. *Organic Flower Gardening*. Emmaus, Pa.: Rodale Press, 1975

Firth, Grace. *A Natural Year*. New York: Simon and Schuster, 1972

Franck, Gertrud. *Companion Planting*. Wellingborough, England: Thorsons Publishing Group, 1983

Galston, Arthur W. *Green Wisdom*. New York: Perigee, 1981

Gershuny, Grace and Joseph Smillie. *The Soul of Soil*. Quebec: Gaia Services, 1986

Hansen, James quoted in "Water Wisdom" by Victoria Mattern in *Organic Gardening* February 1990: 41

Henderson, Peter. *Practical Floriculture*. New York: Judd Company, [1869]

Hill, Stuart B. *Agricultural Chemicals and the Soil.* Paper presented at Chemicals and Agriculture, Problems and Alternatives conference, Fort Qu'Appelle, Saskatchewan, 1977

————. "The pesticide debate" in *Agrologist* 1983, Vol. 12, no. 1

Howard, Robert. *What Makes the Crops Rejoice.* Boston: Little, Brown, 1986

Kruckeberg, Arthur R. *Gardening with Native Plants of the Pacific Northwest.* Vancouver/Toronto: Douglas & McIntyre, 1982

Lee, Albert. *Weather Wisdom,* Chicago: Congdon & Weed, 1976

McHoy, Peter. *Anatomy of a Garden.* London: Marshall Cavendish, 1987

Page, Robin. *Weather Forecasting The Country Way.* Harmondsworth: Penguin, 1987

Riotte, Louise. *Astrological Gardening.* Pownal, Vermont: Garden Way Publishing, 1989

————. *Carrots Love Tomatoes.* Pownal Vermont: Garden Way Publishing, 1975

————. *Roses Love Garlic.* Pownal, Vermont: Garden Way Publishing, 1983

Rubin, Carole. *How to get your lawn & garden off drugs.* Ottawa: Friends of the Earth, 1989

Smith, Miranda and Anna Carr. *Rodale's Garden Insect, Disease & Weed Identification Guide.* Emmaus, Pa.: Rodale Press, 1988

Tompkins, Peter and Christopher Bird. *Secrets of The Soil.* New York: Harper & Row, 1989

Encyclopaedias

The Canadian Encyclopedia. Edmonton: Hurtig, 1988

Encyclopedia of Organic Gardening, The. Emmaus, Pa.: Rodale Press, 1978

Encyclopedia of Natural Insect & Disease Control. Emmaus, Pa.: Rodale Press, 1984

Hortus Third. New York: Macmillan, 1976

Reader's Digest Magic and Medicine of Plants. Montreal/New York: 1986

Wyman, Donald. *Wyman's Gardening Encyclopedia,* 2nd ed. New York: Macmillan, 1986

Periodicals:

Canadian Gardening Magazine
131 Spy Court
Markham, Ont. L3R 5H6
COGnition
25 Sandbar Willoway
Willowdale, Ont. M2J 2B1

Gardenesque
14 Gertrude Place
Toronto, Ont. M4J 1R3
Gardens West
1090 W. 8th Avenue, Box 1680
Vancouver, B.C. V6B 3W8
Harrowsmith
7 Queen Victoria Road
Camden East, Ont. K0K 1J0
The Island Grower
R.R. 4
Sooke, B.C. V0S 1N0
The Journal of the Ontario Rock Garden Society
Box 146
Shelburne, Ont. L0N 1S0
Organic Gardening
33 East Minor St.
Emmaus, Pa. 18098 USA
Wildflower
75 Ternhill Crescent
North York, Ont. M3C 2E4

INDEX
Page numbers in **boldface** indicate illustrations

ABOUT THE AUTHOR

Marjorie Harris is a well-known journalist whose articles have been published in major Canadian magazines. She is the author of eight books including *Sciencescape*, with Dr. David Suzuki and *Everyday Law* with her husband Jack Batten. Her previous gardening book, *THE CANADIAN GARDENER* was a bestseller published to enormous acclaim. Harris is national gardening columnist for the *Globe and Mail*. She has been gardening the same plot of land in Toronto since 1967.

Printed in Canada